Martin Classical Lectures

Martin Classical Lectures

Volume XXIV

The Martin Classical Lectures are delivered
annually at Oberlin College on a foundation
established by his many friends in honor of
Charles Beebe Martin, for forty-five years
a teacher of classical literature and
classical art in Oberlin.

Thucydides
on the
Nature of Power

A. Geoffrey Woodhead

Published for Oberlin College
by Harvard University Press
Cambridge, Massachusetts
1970

Foreword

'SPEECHES measured by the hour', wrote Thomas Jefferson, 'die with the hour'. Fortunately, the lectures founded in honour of Charles Beebe Martin have consistently proved Jefferson wrong, and have acquired so great a reputation in the field of international classical studies that to receive an invitation to deliver them in itself confers an honour and distinction upon the recipient. I am deeply grateful to the Committee administering the Martin Lectures for having invited me to deliver the 1968 series, and to the staff of the Department of Classics at Oberlin College, and their wives, for their generous hospitality during the very pleasant week of my stay on the Oberlin campus. My thanks are due in particular to Professor and Mrs. Charles Murphy, who showed me every kindness.

The lectures have now been translated into book form, with the addition of such documentation as appeared to be helpful and the elaboration in the notes of a few points which could not be argued in the context of the auditorium. I must express my sincere gratitude to the Harvard University Press for their care and patience in dealing with the manuscript, and to Mrs. Greta Blake and Miss Janet Belton for valuable secretarial assistance. Professor A. E. Raubitschek and Mr. G. T. Griffith read much of my material at an early stage and helped me greatly by their comments and criticisms. To them and to other good friends who have shown a helpful interest in the ideas expressed in this book

I am happy to have this opportunity of recording my very grateful thanks.

Just before the lectures were delivered, there died in Cambridge one of the foremost Thucydidean scholars of his generation, whose teaching and friendship have been for me, as for many others, a source of continual guidance and encouragement. It is therefore with a mixture of pleasure and sadness that I dedicate the pages that follow to Sir Frank Adcock, in affectionate memory.

A. G. W.

June 1968

Contents

Introduction

THE Martin Classical Lectures which form the basis of five of the seven chapters which follow were delivered in the middle part of March 1968. Precision in this detail is not without its importance. Any book, or series of lectures, is the child of its time, and reflects not only the background of the world contemporary with it but also the reactions of its author to that world. A knowledge of the events of the period which gave rise to a particular work of scholarship in the field of ancient history, and an acquaintance with the current ideas and modes of thought which shaped the approach of the scholar to his subject, are indispensable to the reader when he seeks to understand and profit from the book in his hands. The ferment of 1848 and its aftermath left their mark on Theodor Mommsen's attitude to the Roman constitutional and social studies to which he devoted himself. That Napoleon III produced a work on Caesar is the more intelligible in the context of the Second Empire. Sir Ronald Syme's *Roman Revolution* is redolent of the nineteen-thirties which gave it birth, and can properly be appreciated only against the setting of the rise of the Third Reich. From Grote to Carcopino and beyond, historians who also have been men of affairs, or who have at least been something more than the prisoners of their study and of their subject, have carried their experience of the world into their interpretation of the epochs which were the object of their historical investigations.

Equally, the considerations which prompted these chapters to take the form they did must be related by the reader to the world of 1967–68, to the America of Lyndon Johnson, the Britain of Harold Wilson, the France of Charles de Gaulle, the China of Mao Tse-tung, the Russia of Leonid Brezhnev and Aleksei Kosygin, and so forth. It is as well for him to be fully conscious of this at the outset.

Nothing 'dates' like a contemporary allusion. There is no need, for an example of the truth of this, to rely on the plays of Aristophanes. It is understandable, although a trifle sad, that the operas of Gilbert and Sullivan, or the adventures of Conan Doyle's hero Sherlock Holmes, begin to need their scholarly footnotes, explaining to new generations ignorant of them the finer points of the dialogue or indeed the everyday matters of the world of the time which author and reader or audience could once take for granted as common ground. Although for the printed page these lectures have been shorn of many of the references of this kind which, at the time of their delivery, sought to add vividness to them and to emphasise their relevance, many still remain. It would be a pity if this were not so, and what is said here would lose much by any attempt to make it appear 'timeless' in its reference. Such readers as may turn to it in future years—readers to whom many of the 'contemporary' matters referred to will already be so much ancient history, as remote as the Peloponnesian War itself—will have no difficulty in reading into it at the appropriate places allusions and parallels from their own society or from events of their own time which will serve to provide an equally cogent emphasis. The points will not be lost thereby, nor their effect substantially impaired.

When the subject under study is Thucydides, this contemporaneity is so much the more easy to achieve. Thucydides speaks with a clear voice to every age, indeed to every decade as its changing circumstances unfold, and with a freshness and a sharpness of relevance which is perennially stimulating. It is generally acknowledged that ancient history must be continually reinterpreted by each generation in the light of its own experience. Histories of Greece succeed one another as requirements and attitudes change, and new interpreters arise to satisfy those needs and attitudes. Thucydides in particular demands and receives perpetual restudy and fresh evaluation as new sets of readers and students bring to him their own changing habits of thought and personal quests for enlightenment. Books about him appear with a frequency discouraging to the professional scholar, who may be understandably lukewarm in his welcome of a further addition to their number. Yet that very frequency is in itself indicative of the need for the illumination which he provides and of the continuing regard for his historical insight. It is a standing acknowledgement of his fundamental importance as a historian of humankind in all ages, a man, in a sense, for all seasons.[1]

That these books on Thucydides may be divided, according to the judgement of those who use them and especially of those who review them, into the good, the bad, and the indifferent does not reflect on the enduring value of their subject. Into whichever of these categories this present work may be adjudged to fall, it does at least claim the merit of laying stress upon this essential relevance and perpetual contemporaneity of Thucydidean study. There are of course those to whom the examination of the later fifth century B.C. constitutes an end in itself—for whom Thucydides, and careful analysis of what he says, are relevant only to a more accurate and comprehensive understanding of the world he describes. It is for them part of the search for the real truth about that sector of human achievement which *le bon Dieu* has enjoined upon them. Such an approach, admittedly *beschränkt,* is all very well in its way; but for most people the real question is that posed at the end of the last chapter of this book—'what is there in it for me?' Every new inquirer, in every age, will find as all have found hitherto that there is indeed something in it for him. Thucydides' work has become in a very real sense the 'possession for all time' he intended it to be, albeit in directions unimagined by him. It is to realise this, and to approach Thucydidean studies in a manner which will accommodate both fifth-century *Wissenschaft* and the immediate environment of the reader, that makes it worth while, in examining Thucydides, to assimilate him to the time in which we live. We may indeed find his greatest service to us in his capacity for such assimilation. In consequence, and *mutatis mutandis,* it is reasonable to suppose that, whenever and wherever they may be read, the considerations that follow, on the nature of power as it appears in Thucydides' pages, are likely to suggest hereafter the same relevance and immediacy which they suggested on those snowy March days in Ohio when they were first presented. At the same time they may represent an examination of an aspect of Thucydides' work with an independent existence which need not stand in debt to the particular lessons it may also convey. It is with this dual purpose that the lectures were originally framed, and it is in the belief that they possess, in this two-fold sense, a potential interest and usefulness to a wider audience that they have been committed to print.

Thucydides on the Nature of Power

Chapter 1

Our opinion of the gods and our knowledge of men lead us to the conclusion that it is a general and necessary law of nature to rule wherever one can. This is not a law we Athenians made ourselves, nor are we the first to act upon it since its establishment. We found it already in existence, and we shall leave it in existence for ever among those who come after us. We are merely acting in accordance with it, and we know that you or anybody else with the same power as that which is now ours would act in exactly the same way.

Thucydides V 105, 2

In the first place, I put for a general inclination of all mankind a perpetual and restless desire of Power after power, that ceaseth only in Death. And the cause of this is not always that a man hopes for a more intensive delight, than he has already attained to; or that he cannot be content with a moderate power; but because he cannot assure the power and means to live well, which he hath present, without the acquisition of more.

Thomas Hobbes, Leviathan XI

> The creatures, see, of flood and field,
> And those that travel on the wind—
> With them no strife can last; they live
>   In peace, and peace of mind.
>
> For why? Because the good old rule
> Sufficeth them, the simple plan,
> That they should take, who have the power,
>   And they should keep who can.
>
> All kinds and creatures stand and fall
> By strength of prowess or of wit.
> 'Tis God's appointment who must sway
>   And who is to submit.

William Wordsworth, Rob Roy's Grave.

Power and the Historian

It is not necessary to teach men to thirst after power.
Men love to hear of their power, but have an extreme disrelish to
be told of their duty.
                    Edmund Burke, *From New to Old Whigs* III 77.

In the summer of 416 b.c., the Athenians determined to obtain control of the island of Melos either by the persuasion of their ambassadors sent to talk to the Melians, or, if that method failed, by force. The general course of the negotiations, which in the event failed to persuade the Melians and were followed by a successful siege, was recorded by the historian Thucydides.[1] The source or veracity of his information it is not my intention to consider. What is significant for this context is that he uses the occasion to expound, in the form of a dialogue which was later and most successfully adopted for philosophical exposition by Plato, what he sees as the underlying principles of the Athenian action. The remark of the Athenian envoys which appears at the head of the introductory quotations is familiar and important. It is because it is important that it is familiar. It may be, as Ernest Barker once observed, that Thucydides is here writing more as a philosopher than as an historian, and that he makes his figures 'explicitly profess the principles which. . . they themselves perhaps,

3

after the manner of politicians, veiled in a discreet cloud of respectable words'.[2] Nevertheless we must concede that the words used here are frank and honest, and the open expression of them in such a situation is by no means inconceivable. Thucydides, as an historian of men's actions and motives for action, could be writing not as a theorist but as a recorder of what was said or what could well have been said in the actual negotiations.

Beside the quotation from Thucydides' Melian Dialogue I set an equally famous quotation from the *Leviathan* of Thomas Hobbes—what K. C. Brown[3] has called his 'splendid and terrible dictum', in which the Athenians' sentiments, as Thucydides describes them, are set echoing in a new environment and to a new purpose. There is no doubt of the effect that Thucydides, flowing through such channels as these, has exercised on modern political thought; nor is there doubt of the appositeness of the questions raised by him, and by those he has influenced, for the second half of the twentieth century. It was not for nothing that Hobbes himself translated Thucydides' *History;* and Leo Strauss, in his *Thoughts on Machiavelli,* was right to remark of that author also that contemporary readers are reminded, by his teaching, of Thucydides.[4] Both Machiavelli and Hobbes were deeply impressed by the character of sovereignty and its inherent rightness; and because it is of itself both natural and right the possessor of it may, by nature and right, or by natural right, exercise it while he has it to the fullest of its possibilities. The man who does so (or in Thucydidean terms we might say the state that does so) attains to a deserved felicity. Nietzsche, with the example of Napoleon before him, regarded the successful wielder of power as the superman, and considered the enhancement of his power-consciousness as a proper criterion of truth. Thucydides, in his approach to the problem of political power and its effect on history in general, through the mirror of his *History* in particular, thus stands at the beginning of a long development of historico-philosophic thought. To go back to him and to consider what his approach was has, in consequence, been relevant in every age, and is no less urgently relevant in our own, when the exercise of the kind of power which he described involves new dangers and new dimensions.

It is regrettably easy for an inquiry into that approach to become diverted into a preoccupation with Thucydides' political attitudes and predilections in specific areas or issues with which he is concerned. It is fashionable to enquire in narrower terms, for instance, about the historian's endorsement of Pericles and his régime in Athens, and his hostility towards the post-Periclean democracy, or to study his ambivalent attitude towards the Athenian Empire, which he alleged to be unpopular with those peoples subject to it and the maintenance of which he seems at times to admire and at times to condemn. It is noted and discussed that he expressed explicit approval[5] of the moderate oligarchy of the Five Thousand which replaced the democracy for not quite ten months in the years 411–410. Interesting though his likes and dislikes are, it is equally arguable that what Thucydides' personal opinions were about the manifestations he describes are of less consequence than the actual descriptions he gives. Such questions as I have alluded to, though indeed worthy of study and attention, are less apposite than might be thought. As an example, we may select that problem of the Athenian Empire and Thucydides' judgement on it, about which there has been a great deal of discussion in the last fifteen years, with thesis and counter-thesis propounded with some regularity in the learned journals.[6] Was the Empire acceptable or not to the Athenian allies? Thucydides gives the clue to their real status, as he saw it, when he calls them ὑπήκοοι, 'subjects'.[7] This is a statement of fact, or his view of the fact; we need not interpret it as conveying a condemnatory judgement. Twice Thucydides emphasises the unpopularity of the dominion of Athens—unpopular with those already subject to it and feared by those who might become so.[8] The received tradition accepts this view as an objectively accurate one. Those who have defended it against challenge with regard to its accuracy have hastened to reinforce their claim of its acceptability as a piece of allegedly independent observation, by appealing to further arguments on its moral justification. This, however, introduces the further implication of the acceptability of the Empire not only to the susceptibilities of Thucydides but also to our own, and proceeds to raise the issue of Empire in general and of the use of power to obtain and maintain it. The field of vision must in consequence be widened to take in the study of power itself in the context of Thucydides and his *History*.

The controversy on the popularity of the Athenian Empire, interesting as it has been, has served only to polarise opposing viewpoints and has effectively led only to a better realisation that there are more tenable viewpoints than one. It has not produced any clearer vision of the reality of Athenian control, for that was clear enough. What Thucydides thought, or thought that others thought, and why he thought it does not affect that reality. Nor is it affected by moral arguments for or against Athenian methods of administration to which we may have recourse. Not only is there doubt of their relevance, but there is also a serious danger that we may introduce into them modern attitudes to 'colonialism' and 'imperialism' which would be out of place in the ancient context. The Athenian Empire meant different things to different people, then as now. Thucydides as a contemporary has suggested its meaning for *him,* although in the course of this record its meaning for others also appears—for scholars on both sides of the controversy I have mentioned draw supporting data from him. But Athenian power existed and exercised itself independently of its observers, obeying principles which stood whether they approved or disapproved. Approval or disapproval, whether Thucydides' or the Athenian allies' or our own, is beside the point.

The Athenian Empire is only one manifestation of power in action in Thucydides' world. What we are concerned with now, therefore, is not the historian's personal attitude to such manifestations, to political systems like democracy or oligarchy, to political personalities like Pericles or Cleon, or to political institutions like popular law-courts or representative councils. It is a concern rather with his attitude to the nature of the power which those systems or those individuals or those organs of government exercised, and with his interpretation of the contexts in which they exercised it. It is indeed true that we cannot entirely divorce the concept of power from the practicalities of the situation, from the people who acquired or used power, or from the systems and institutions which were the framework or the vehicle of that exercise. It is in fact through Thucydides' treatment of the separate issues or manifestations of power that we have to elicit his attitude towards the principle and the exercise of power itself. For instance, there were and are in practice inhibiting factors in the use of power, as J. R. Lucas has correctly argued[9] and as Thucydides equally correctly depicts. Since, from the nature of our evidence, we are constrained to see all the issues and manifestations largely through Thucydides' eyes we cannot cut ourselves off entirely from Thucydides' analysis of them, appealing only to the facts as he appears to state them.

This consideration may be taken a stage further. For example, we have to bear in mind that there may be a relationship, whether of conflict or otherwise, between Thucydides the recorder and Thucydides the analyst.[10] We must not only watch how he describes situations in which power is discussed or exercised, as in the Melian Dialogue, but we must also observe how he phrases his descriptions, what words he uses and the connotations of those words.[11] And in so doing it emerges that we must investigate whether to Thucydides the recorder and Thucydides the analyst we must also add Thucydides the judge. To put a simple dilemma, to which I referred earlier—is Thucydides reporting what the Athenians at Melos (or Athenians in general) in fact thought about the character of power, as I stated? Or is he expressing what he believes to have been a theory of power on which they acted but which, as Barker thought, they would have hesitated openly to acknowledge, or the reality of which they did not comprehend? Or is Thucydides using the situation in order to enunciate, by this unusual method, his own personal theory, unrelated to what anyone else in fact thought or said or did? In any choice we may make among these possibilities, we are tempted to ask a further question—is Thucydides explicitly or implicitly condemning such a doctrine as he expresses in relation to Athens' pressure on Melos? The possibilities are not mutually exclusive and may indeed be combined. Thucydides can report and, in the manner of his reporting, criticise at the same time, as he does for example at the time of the Spartan request for peace in 425 B.c., when he reports the Spartan arguments and omits the counter-arguments of the Athenians.[12] Plainly stated, it is the contention of this chapter that, in the fact of power and in the rightness of its exercise, Thucydides is reporting and no more, and that his attitude to power, like power itself in its nature, is neutral.

The trouble is—and this is to some extent why so much effort is expended in diagnosing what Thucydides' own opinions are—that *we* do not want Thucydides to be neutral, and we do not want power to be neutral either. We want to model the great historian in our own image, to see him as moral in the condemnation of power and its exercise, because we ourselves prefer to regard power as intrinsically immoral, as a vehicle of corruption. The connexion between power and morality, ancient as it is and examined with a clarity still unsurpassed by the Greek tragic dramatists, has emerged as one of the great issues of our time which occupies and troubles those who give thought to public affairs more perhaps than, in their concern for specific problems and remedies, they sometimes realise. Now whether the acquisition and exercise of power, in the sense to which I have referred, is indeed to be regarded by us as a moral proceeding, and whether this takes place in our own time or in the fifth century B.C., seems to be beside the point of our inquiry. We shall return to the question of morality of power in the fifth century in the last chapter, and whether Thucydides contaminated his concept of power with a moral judgement about it we shall consider later in this one. What we must be careful to do is to keep ourselves and our own judgements out of it. It is quite irrelevant whether we think the Athenians were good men or bad men to have enunciated the doctrine to the Melians that they did; and it is the more irrelevant if, as is inescapable, any conclusion we make, one way or the other, is to be based on what *we* regard as moral.

We must accept, I think, that the problem of the relationship between public and private morality preoccupies us in a way that was alien to the world of Thucydides. That there was this kind of problem under discussion we know well, but it took a different form; it was concerned with a clash of differing authoritative claims on the individual rather than with a conflict between authoritative claim on the one side and the absence of claim, connoting in the modern view freedom, on the other, which is the way in which it presents itself to us. The possession of power, and the employment of the authority derived from it, were not questioned by the Greeks as they are by us. The quotation from the Melian Dialogue with which we began acknowledges them, and it was not controverted. The Athenians expect that they may one day be sufferers from the law's application, just as at the time of the conquest of Melos they were its beneficiaries; but they do not complain that there is something wrong with this.[13] They will not use terms such as that their action is 'right' or 'just', save insofar as the privileges of using these terms is conferred on them by the possession of power. Power itself, that is to say, is neutral in its character. It may be just according to the point of view of the person so describing it, but the description does not affect its essence. The Athenians enunciated the law of nature and the gods. The existence of that law is accepted by Thucydides, and by Machiavelli, and by Hobbes. It is we who do not accept it, and who, since the time of Hobbes, have sought ways and means of circumnavigating his conclusions.[14] Our attitude to the law is as a result ambivalent. It is through Hobbes that we may see how the ambivalence comes about. 'Whether men will or not', he says (as the Athenians at Melos more or less said), 'they must be subject to the Divine Power'; and again, 'it comes to pass that we are obliged to obey God in His natural kingdom'.[15] In a world which, though largely pagan, derives its general concept of morality and its motivation from the Hebrew concept of God and the Christian concept of the divine revelation, we cannot reconcile the divine law as we wish nowadays to understand it with the divine law as the Athenians expressed it or as Hobbes modified it. Thus our own accepted habits of thought, and our reactions to expressions based on those habits of thought, tend to hamper us in any appreciation of what Thucydides is telling us.

Let us take a simple example. After the failure of the negotiations in December 1966 on board *HMS Tiger* between the British Prime Minister and the head of the 'illegal régime' in Rhodesia, Mr. Harold Wilson in his condemnation of Mr. Ian Smith observed that Smith and his party were 'merely bent on clinging to power'. This, as he made explicit by the choice of his language and the tone of his voice, was a bad thing and the men who sought to hold on to the power that they had were bad men. To Thucydides and his contemporaries as he portrays them this would have meant nothing. Of course people sought power; of course they kept their grip on it, or tried their best to do so, when they had it. This was a natural phenomenon, and a neutral phenomenon, neither good nor bad. And it still is.

It is in fact the stuff of history. 'Crowns and thrones may perish', runs the hymn, 'kingdoms rise and wane'. Power is let slip by one, only to pass into the hands of another, whether we speak of individuals or of nations. If we may look to the Melian Dialogue for Thucydides the recorder, reporting what he saw as the current concept of power on the basis of which the Athenians acted, we may look to the opening of Book I, the so-called *Archaeology,* for Thucydides the analyst, analysing what were the factors of power and of its generation in Greece. Too many people in reading Thucydides pass rapidly over those first eighteen chapters as merely prefatory; they are in fact integral to any consideration of Thucydides' thought about the factors controlling his own world. What were the essentials of power in Greece? Centralisation, Thucydides says, makes for power, and the accumulated inheritance of Agamemnon gave that king a supremacy at the time of the Trojan War which, by implication, parallels the supremacy enjoyed in the fifth century by the centralised empire of the Athenians.[16] Sea-power, he points out, was no less contributory to Agamemnon's domination, and had been demonstrated from the time of Minos onwards as the key to leadership in Greece—which the Athenians still found it to be. Furthermore Agamemnon collected his armament 'not so much by good-will (χάρις) as by fear'. Power, that it, causes other people to stand in fear or awe of its possessor. But although the expedition of Agamemnon was more formidable than any expedition Greece had known hitherto, it was inferior to the fame and tradition about it that the poets had given it, and was relatively small in size. Why was this? Not so much from lack of men as from lack of resources, says Thucydides.[17] On both counts the comparable position of Athens springs to mind—that Athens whose power was such, he later affirms, that all cities were in the position either of wanting to get rid of her domination or of being afraid that they might fall under it, who had inspired in Sparta such fear that this was the 'truest cause' of Sparta's decision for war,[18] and whose resources were so great that Pericles dwells on them at length, in that well-known Chapter 13 of Book II, with pride and with emphasis.[19] These were the trump cards of power, and Athens held them all.

But Power is not static. For one thing, it has an effect on the holder of it, and becomes a vested interest with him. He cannot let it go without hazard to himself and to the standard of personal well-being which it has enabled him to attain. So Pericles rightly says to the Athenians 'the dominion you exercise is like a tyranny, which . . . it is dangerous to let go'.[20] 'Loss of empire is one of the issues at stake, and danger from the hatred which your dominion has incurred; from that dominion it is too late to withdraw'. Indeed, the possessor of power certainly feels no inclination to withdraw from what I earlier described, following Hobbes, as a deserved felicity.[21] The Athenians, so Thucydides tells us, clearly regarded themselves as deserving it.

They pointed to their record of leadership and service to Greece.[22] They had been foremost in defeating the Persians; the other Greeks had put themselves under their hegemony; they had shown courage, resolution, ability. 'We have done nothing extraordinary', say the Athenians in the Spartan assembly, 'nothing contrary to human nature in accepting a dominion when it was offered us and in refusing to give it up'.[23] They claim, furthermore, that the Spartans would have done precisely the same had they gone on leading the Greeks against Persia and not, by defaulting, let the Athenians into the position they vacated. It was a fair claim, for after their victory in 404 this is precisely what the Spartans did.

The effect of power on its holder is indeed not that it corrupts him. The famous dictum of Lord Acton, that power tends to corrupt, does not stand up to close scrutiny,[24] and even if it be introduced into the discussion it would be necessary to reject it with emphasis as irrelevant to the Thucydidean context, because it introduces that very moral implication we are doing our best to avoid. We should beware of 'loaded' words of this kind. It is sufficient to say that the possession of power predisposes its possessor to a certain set of reactions and to a certain approach to policy. In fact the Athenians go on to tell the Spartans quite expressly what the effect on them has been; and this also is echoed, in some part, by Pericles in another situation. 'Three powerful motives prevent us from giving up our position—honour, apprehension, and self-interest' ($\tau\iota\mu\acute{\eta}$, $\delta\acute{\epsilon}os$, and $\mathring{\omega}\phi\epsilon\lambda\acute{\iota}a$). The retention of power is vital not only because of the danger at the hands of those at whose expense power is exercised, but because it is profitable to those who enjoy it, and because they see their dignity enhanced by it. Its honours bring burdens, as Pericles notes in his last recorded speech, but the Athenians must not shrink from the burdens because they must reasonably be expected to support the position of honour in which they take pride.[25]

'Pride' is a word to which we should pay particular attention. David Grene called the first edition of his study in the political philosophy of Thucydides and Plato 'Man in his Pride'. The rather catchpenny title, abandoned in the second edition, was drawn from a poem of W. B. Yeats. It could have been elicited from Thucydides himself, or from Hobbes, who significantly uses it in a context which points us to the third aspect of Thucydides and the concept of power which we must study. If power itself is neutral, and the factors which produce it are neutral, and the factors that may take it away (like *tyche,* or fortune, to which we shall return in a later context) are equally neutral, there is one point at which the morality of the wielder of power is liable to intervene. And in recording the event the morality of the recorder is liable to intervene no less. From Thucydides the recorder and Thucydides the analyst we thus progress to Thucydides the judge. It is *how* the power is exercised, whether by honourable or dishonourable means and for honourable or dishonourable ends, that introduces the new factor. We have already seen that power bestows honour, and that man takes pride in honour. What adds honour to power is when a man who might use power arbitrarily actually uses it with justice.[26] 'Those who really deserve praise', say the Athenians at Sparta, 'are the people who, while human enough to enjoy power, nevertheless pay more attention to justice than they are compelled to do by their situation'.

The aristocratic man, or the magnanimous man, according to Hobbes, disdains to owe his life or his prosperity to underhanded or shameful or fraudulent acts. He possesses what appears from Hobbes's description as a *sancta superbia*. He desires power and fears death as other men do, but he puts honour above life. 'That which gives to human actions the relish of Justice, is a certain noblenesse or gallantnesse of courage, rarely found, by which a man scorns to be beholding for the contentment of his life to fraud or breach of promise.' [27] Such a man has power, of course, but his exercise of it brings him respect, and respect brings honour, in which he takes pride. He is in fact the 'gallant man' or 'the man of pride'. One may hark back to the Athenians' justification of their dominion and wonder, basically, why they bothered to justify it. If might was its own right, they need not apologise. [28] But *that,* to be fair, they were not attempting to claim. It was unnecessary for them to adopt a Thrasymachean attitude in this sense, for there was and is basically no need, if the operation of the laws of power are followed through, to attempt to substitute the word 'right' for the word 'might', to equate δύναμις with τὸ δίκαιον, as Thrasymachus did. It is an unnecessary elaboration, *se si guarda al fine.* 'It is not right to succeed', as J. H. Hexter has observed; [29] 'it is merely success to succeed'. In a very different context, P. A. Brunt has suggested that something of this sort is nearer to the Athenian position. [30] 'It is the way the world goes; might does not create right but excludes it.'

But the Athenians were not, or not quite, saying this either, on Thucydides' reckoning. They certainly agreed that τὸ δικάζεσθαι, justificatory pleading, was not strictly necessary, for pragmatically and by divine law there were rulers and ruled, and rulers naturally ruled and those who were ruled had, correspondingly, to obey. This involves more than the 'ethical nihilism' of a Callicles or a Thrasymachus, as Plato depicts it in the *Gorgias* or in Book I of the *Republic*.[31] It does in the event introduce moral issues where Callicles and Thrasymachus, taking the Melian Dialogue to an extreme by the misuse of the terminology of morality, deny them utterly. The Athenians regarded their attack on Melos as justified by the position of power which they had achieved and had deserved to achieve. They could indeed have advanced the δικαιώματα in which they believed, and they refer to them at the beginning of the debate, for they had not renounced them. They were, however, well aware that the Melians would not accept them as a compelling reason for their own immediate subjection, and so they moved on, in consequence, to arguments which would have a greater cogency with Melos. Thucydides, in describing this realistic procedure, does not discount the basic validity of the δικαιώματα, which are here left unelaborated but which are more fully expounded elsewhere. They constitute a 'morality of pride' (or in Hobbes's term 'gallantry') which he portrays the Athenians and Pericles as accepting and which, in the vehicle of the Funeral Speech,[32] he evidently accepts himself. In accepting it, he accepts also a code of morals in which keeping one's word, being generous, and acting according to the virtue of justice are higher in the scale of values than life, wealth, or any of the material good things which the possessor of power may command. Thus it cannot be said of him, as G. P. Gooch remarked of Machiavelli[33] and as we might plausibly say of Callicles or Thrasymachus, that he is 'radically unfair to mankind'.

I referred earlier to Leo Strauss' remark that in reading Machiavelli one is reminded of Thucydides; at this point the quotation might profitably be continued.[34] 'Contemporary readers find in both authors the same "realism", that is to say, the same denial of the power of the gods or of justice and the same sensitivity to harsh necessity and elusive chance. Yet Thucydides never calls into question the intrinsic superiority of nobility to baseness, a superiority that shines forth particularly when the noble is destroyed by the base. Therefore, Thucydides' *History* arouses in the reader a sadness which is never aroused by Machiavelli's books . . .'. Strauss seems to me right in judging that 'the noble' and 'the base' are indeed recognised by Thucydides as concepts against which he himself judges actions or regards action as to be judged. For him they are concepts with meaning, not words which a man may use and abuse with the attribution of such meanings as he cares to give them. But I do *not* believe that he denies the power of justice. He does not, indeed, seem to feel that justice exists as an independent force, that somehow the good men will triumph and the bad men will come to grief because the world is just and the laws which govern the growth, development, and transfer of power are just. Rather does he see justice as a concept, like the noble and the base, which motivates some men in a lofty sense, and which others debase for their own purposes and employ as a cloak for less creditable motives.

Not that whether power, once acquired, was justly acquired is really apposite in given circumstances. Pericles faces this problem in a quotation which, again, was left incomplete in an earlier context. The facts of power cannot be gainsaid, once the holder of power does hold and exercise it. 'The dominion you exercise is like a tyranny', said Pericles.[35] 'Perhaps it was contrary to justice (ἄδικον) to have acquired it, but it is certainly dangerous to let it go'. In other words, the matter of δίκη in its acquisition is ancient history, and, though it is disputable to some, such a dispute is irrelevant in face of the facts of the present time. The Athenians themselves, as we have seen, did *not* think the matter disputable; *they* regarded their acquisition of their dominion as their due, at least if we may judge by the words put into the mouths of their representatives at Sparta.[36] But there may have been some who, confronted by the Peloponnesian War, were beginning to wonder about this question, and Pericles' answer to them is clear. It is no good theorising about moral issues which have shaped present facts. You have to face the present facts as they are; and whatever the rights and wrongs about the earlier moral issues the contemporary *facts* of power, being neutral, have to be treated as such.

The intervention of justice as a concept at this point is an important element in the discussion, and it receives its fullest treatment—the final phase of a long argument—in Plato's *Republic*. When Plato makes Thrasymachus proclaim that justice is nothing more than what each man decides to think it is, and more specifically that it boils down to a name given by the powerful man to his own self-interest, he is picking up what Thucydides had already observed in the third of his *loci classici* on the character of power. It forms part of the general background of thought in Thucydides' world—a view in vogue among the intelligentsia, though not, as will be suggested in the final chapter, one which the man in the street would feel comfortable in endorsing. It faced Thucydides with a particular problem to which we must now return.

I used earlier in this chapter a phrase to the effect that sovereignty possesses an inherent rightness. The attempt to acquire it is natural; its retention and exercise need no justification. But a man must himself go bail for the *manner* in which he retains and exercises it, and if we use words like justice, honour, dignity, and so forth in the process we are not at liberty to juggle their meanings to suit ourselves, on the pattern advocated by Thrasymachus in the first book of Plato's *Republic*. Thrasymachus' doctrine more or less amounted to the thesis that might is right, or at least that the powerful man or state can exercise might and give it the name right, and that he is fully entitled so to do. A. W. Gomme once said that we should not be so naïve as to think that Thucydides believed this.[37] But I have already urged that Thucydides' own beliefs are beside the point, and our possible naïveté need not trouble us. In any case, his *dynamis* is devoid of any adjectival elaboration in moral value-terms like 'right' or 'unjust'. It is the confounding of morally and emotionally evocative words with the reality of the situation which is morally reprehensible, and that is in fact, as Thucydides is well aware, what people do. It is this that he emphasises in what I have just described as the third of the *loci classici* on the character and exercise of power. In the first we have seen Thucydides recording the facts about the nature of power, in the second we have seen him analysing the facts in the acquisition of power and the motives which, once it has been acquired, lead to its retention. Now we find Thucydides the judge not merely reporting but also con-

demning what men do when their motives and methods for
seeking to acquire or retain power are bad, when human
nature disregards law, moderation and justice, and when
words and ideas of good moral content are used in place of,
or as a cloak for, ideas and actions unworthy of them. This
locus classicus is of course the passage describing and com-
menting upon the revolution in Corcyra.[38] In this situation
the 'morality of pride' disappears, and we are indeed faced
with the application of the nihilism of Callicles or Thrasymachus. Thucydides tells us that, given the right sort of ex-
acerbating circumstances, this sort of thing does happen, and
we should be warned for the future. It is part of the character of power that other people, who have not got it, want
it; they try to obtain it if they can, and even if they cannot
they dislike and envy the possessor of it, whatever his merits.
Phthonos ($\phi\theta\acute{o}\nu os$), a composite of envy and rivalry, is
inevitably awakened. When Pericles and the Athenians at
Sparta both observe that Athenian dominion in Greece has
aroused *echthos* ($\check{\epsilon}\chi\theta os$), 'enmity', this is a natural consequence of their power—it does not mean that they have
done anything wrong, unjust, or cruel in its exercise. And
both *phthonos* and *echthos* are, in basis, aspects of the
respect or fear which power inspires. The powerful man or
state must expect to have his enemies, who will cover their
enmity and envy by saying that they stand for justice, equality before the law, peace, humanity, morality itself, and so
forth. The 'fine phrases', the $\mathring{o}\nu\acute{o}\mu a\tau a$ $\kappa a\lambda \acute{a}$, which the
Athenians warned the Melians to leave strictly out of the
argument,[39] appear in this context in full force. Thucydides
knew that in essence they have nothing to do with the character of power, and that in the exercise of power there are

motivating factors which have no connexion with them. But the good man looks to a moral code outside and beyond these; and the bad man, knowing that the phraseology of the code conveys a 'good' connotation with which he wishes to associate himself, misuses it for his own ends. It is this misuse which Thucydides criticises in the Corcyrean stasis; not the conflict itself, which is a natural process. Similarly at Melos it is the misuse of victory which is to be reproved, not the imposition of Athenian power on the Melians, which was not contrary to right or to justice according to the interpretation of these terms that we have seen to be valid.

It is perhaps possible to illustrate Thucydides' attitude to power and its exercise, by way of summing up the points I have been trying to make, by attempting to suggest how Thucydides might have tackled one of the great problems of contemporary history, productive on every side of a tremendous amount of emotion and passion and troubles of conscience—the war in Vietnam.[40] Even when that war has ceased to be contemporary, it will still be illustrative and instructive whenever the issues of power and its use are under discussion. How might Thucydides have analysed the varying reactions to the unhappy events in Southeast Asia? In the first place, we may suggest, Thucydides might have observed, after an initial factual statement of events, that the real issues at stake tended to be increasingly clouded on both sides by propaganda, catchwords, and emotional thinking. In historical analysis the heart is the enemy of the head, as he well knew. He knew too that the clever man of affairs prefers to work on the emotions as more vulnerable, and if he can set fire to popular passions (whatever 'side' people in fact take) he has won half his battle. Thucydides might have posited, I suggest, that there are four reasons on the basis of which the Americans met with criticism, more particularly outside their own country, for their undertaking in Vietnam. In the first place they were in possession of so much power that they were the people to whom weaker states under pressure tended to look for aid. To possess so much power was and is in itself widely thought to be immoral and an affront to humanity. Secondly, it was held against them that, having such power, they in fact intervened. Thirdly, it was asserted that their intervention was made and maintained for entirely selfish ends. Finally, it was objected that, whatever the nature of their ends, their methods (for instance that of bombing North Vietnam) must be regarded as reprehensible. If the historian *had* broken the problem down into those four elements, what would have been his comment, explicit or implied? On the first, that the Americans possessed such great power, he has given us his answer in the *Archaeology* and in other passages already quoted. He could have observed that the Americans fulfilled all the requirements for power—centralisation, resources in men and money, military strength, all productive of respect and fear. The effect of this on others could only be to arouse hatred and envy, and on the Americans themselves to enhance dignity, honour, and a determination to retain their position. Thus they had power, which is a natural phenomenon, and others reviled them for it, which is also a natural phenomenon. The others (as is again natural) used moral terms in which to express their dislike, even though the fact of power has no moral connotation.

We may thus pass to the second objection, the fact that the Americans did indeed intervene in Vietnam on the basis of their undoubted power to do so. 'But', Thucydides might point out, 'of course they did'. Power, as I have said, is not static; it must defend itself where it feels itself threatened, and it must expand if it does not feel itself threatened. Power is useless unless it is exercised. Indeed it only expresses itself or fulfils itself when it is exercised—whether in action or in imposing itself without the necessity of action. The 'second objection' thus proves to be without substance, on Thucydides' reckoning. So it is only when we examine the third objection, the consideration of the ends of action, that Thucydides might even begin to find anything worthy of discussion, anything of validity in the adverse reactions we have envisaged. Here he might well say, as he made the Athenians say, that American δέος, τιμή, and ὠφελία— apprehensions, honour, and self-interest—were all undoubtedly involved. A speech might be given, in the course of his analysis, to the United States representative at the United Nations assembly, in which the speaker might note how much America had done in the past for the defence and salvation of the free world (thus advancing the claim of merit); he might state with correctness, sincerity, and conviction that *eleutheria,* freedom, was the goal of action, and that one must help friends who are wronged and who call upon one for aid. Putting all these considerations together, he might then claim that they are all compatible with the demands of justice, and that it is the part of the good man, and of the good nation, to use power in conjunction with justice. Thucydides could then have followed this, had he felt so inclined, with his own comment, that on analysis he believed these American motives of self-interest to have been allied to a genuine altruism (that is, that the Americans were seriously afraid of the spread of Communism as a danger to themselves and their spheres of interest, but that they also allied to their fear a real wish to help friends and harm enemies). If Thucydides' judgement lay in another direction, he might remark or imply in his phraseology, that self-interest was being concealed under a specious cloak of altruism. But in neither judgement would he have found it reprehensible that self-interest was involved. He would regard that as wholly natural and to be expected, and he would give the United States government extra credit if he thought that they had gone out of their way to act with justice and with consideration for the general good of more people than themselves.

It is on the fourth objection, the means to the end, *how* their power was exercised, that Thucydides might possibly feel called upon to allow considerations which we might characterize as moral considerations to enter the matter. Callicles and Thrasymachus, as we have seen, would not. They would regard all means as legitimate once the three previous points had been agreed. Cleon would have argued for the expediency, legitimate or not, of all possible means. Thucydides might react variously. He might in a speech allotted to them make the Americans say, with the Athenians, that it is the law of nature for them to impose their strength on their adversaries by all and every means, and he could well leave it at that, recording their sentiments and saying no more. He might simply set down the fact that North Vietnam was repeatedly bombed from the air, just as he records, for instance, Sparta's stern treatment of neutral merchant seamen, and make no further observation. Or he might add the reflection, as he does in the case of Corcyra, that war is a stern teacher. He might make some spokesman say, as he makes Cleon say, that, whatever the rights and wrongs may be, if the Americans proposed to defend their power, then, rightly or wrongly, they had to take all means to defend it. He might argue, adopting the view of Nietzsche, that the art of government is beyond good and evil, that the words 'just' and 'unjust', δίκαιον and ἄδικον, cannot even be used of the acts of warfare itself, if the war itself is δίκαιον in relation to the state waging it.[41] He might then add, if he felt it a justified observation, that in the course of prolonged violence or tumult the currency of the words used to express what is just or unjust, right or wrong, tends to become debased. All of these approaches to such a situation are visible in Thucydides, all are commendable and acceptable, and all are in some sense factual, that is, matters of record, or analytical of a possible point of view. What, if any, Thucydides' own final judgement might be we cannot tell; or at least we can only assess for ourselves on our reading of him. We might not find such a judgement our judgement; we might not even find it apposite or profitable to look for it; and I have suggested that such a search may well be an irrelevancy. At the least we are obliged to beware of extracting from him a judgement in our terms that we should wish to have, just because we want it as support for our own attitudes arrived at independently on the basis of our own principles.

In this chapter I have sought to establish certain propositions about Thucydides and his approach to the problem of power in history and in his *History*. In his treatment of states and of individuals we shall see, as we proceed, the points which I have tried to stress further exemplified— power described and illustrated as the object of effort, held and retained by those who have it, envied and hated by those who do not have it, but in itself characterless and without moral content. We shall see its transfer from one man or state to another conditioned by the factors analyzed in the *Archaeology,* the analysis which underlies the development of events in the historical period of which Thucydides writes. Lastly, we shall find that the historian from time to time intervenes with his own value judgements in order to characterize, as he sees them, the actions and methods of men operating within the framework of that divine and human law of power which the Athenians enunciated at Melos. This, in a sense, despite himself, for he gives the appearance of doing his best, I believe, to avoid real emotional involvement, and this in turn conveys that impression of objectivity which has so greatly impressed and frequently misled those who have studied him. For, nevertheless, in writing what happened, and in inquiring why, he could not ultimately stand aside from evaluating how.

It has been acknowledged of Thomas Hobbes that he makes three types of statement relating to human behaviour —descriptive, hypothetical, and imperative. 'Sometimes he tells us what men do', as Plamenatz expresses it,[42] 'and at other times what they would do if they knew what was best for them; and he also tells them to do what is best for them'. In the case of Thucydides we have also diagnosed three types of statement. He shares with Hobbes only the descriptive element, for he is not concerned to be prescriptive nor ever presumes to be so. Thus for the Hobbesian 'hypothetical' and 'imperative' we may, in the case of Thucydides, substitute 'analytical' and 'critical'. It is indeed the 'why' and the 'how' which he explores in the use of power and in the reactions of men, and in varying contexts we shall follow his exploration.

> When the one great scorer comes
>   to write against your name,
> He notes, not that you lost or won,
>   but how you played the game.

Thucydides does more than the great scorer, for he is also prepared to note that you lost or won, and why you achieved the victory or suffered the defeat. But how you played the game is a theme which drew him irresistibly—and nowhere more than in his evaluation of the Athenian democracy. It is to that democracy, and the power it enjoyed, that we shall next turn our attention.

Chapter 2

There are those who will say that democracy is neither a sensible nor an equitable system, but that those who have the money are also the best rulers. But I say, first, that what is meant by the *demos* is the whole people, whereas an oligarchy is only a section of it, and in the second place that the wealthy are the best people for looking after money, but the best people for giving counsel are the most intelligent people, while it is the many who are best at listening to the various arguments and judging between them. And all alike, whether taken separately by classes or all together, enjoy their fair shares in a democratic state.

Thucydides VI 39, 1

Democratic power recognises no other authority in Society than itself, and claims always to go just as far as the General Will carries it. But this Power, if there is no stopping it, is on the other hand eminently open to be wooed and won.

B. de Jouvenel, *Le Pouvoir,* 225

The Common people are always impressed by appearances and results.

Machiavelli, *Il Principe* 18

Nor is the people's judgement always true;
The most may err as grossly as the few.
John Dryden, *Absalom and Achitophel,* Pt. I, ll. 778–9

A perfect democracy is . . . the most shameless thing in the world.
Edmund Burke, *Reflections on the Revolution in France*

Power and the People

IN the winter of the year 499/8 B.C., Aristagoras the tyrant of Miletus, who was trying to organise a revolt of the Greeks in Ionia against their Persian overlords, went to Greece on a mission to secure assistance for his project, visiting first Sparta and then Athens. Herodotus tells the story, with a good many interruptions for digressions of one kind and another, in his fifth book. At Sparta, Aristagoras interviewed King Cleomenes, who was at first impressed with him, but with the help of a precocious remark by Cleomenes' little daughter Gorgo and of his own bad presentation of his case he was ultimately sent packing. Later, at Athens, he spoke to the assembled citizens and, we are told, 'promised everything that came into his head, until at last he succeeded in getting the aid he required'. 'Apparently', adds Herodotus, 'it is easier to impose upon a crowd than upon an individual, for Aristagoras, who had failed to impose upon Cleomenes, had no difficulty with thirty thousand Athenians'.[1] The observation seems to be Herodotus' own, and in this point Thucydides, who found fault with him on several matters, must have felt himself wholeheartedly in agreement with his great predecessor. For it is generally acknowledged, mentioned in all the books which deal with these things, and needing no elaboration now, that Thucydides had no affection for the radical democracy of the Athens of his day.[2] He is explicit in his condemnation of it. He thought it a bad system of government, incompetent and irresponsible, the follies of which were the direct cause of Athens' downfall in the Peloponnesian War. Power in the hands of the people, the *demos* or *plethos,* was the worst kind of πολιτεία, 'mode of government' or 'constitution', that could be devised. Plato in the *Republic* at least regards it as a form of government preferable to tyranny, to which it was so often the threshold.[3] But Thucydides, who is not dealing in theories but is surveying practice, is at pains to remark that the tyranny of the Peisistratids in Athens had been temperate and beneficial—neither of which adjectives could possibly be applied in his view to developed democracy. The two words which Thucydides specifically applies to Peisistratus' rule are ἀρετή (*virtue* or *capability*) and ξύνεσις (*intelligence*)[4]—and there are no higher words of praise for character in his vocabulary than these. As a parallel text, as it were, to Herodotus' story of Aristagoras it would doubtless have been possible to select that statement of Alcibiades at Sparta, when he had arrived there in 415 as an exile, to the effect that concerning Athenian democracy he could say nothing new about a system which was universally reckoned to be an absurdity.[5] But I have chosen instead a passage from the same book (VI) which for once allows Thucydides to appear as saying something nice about democracy. At least, if it is taken by itself, out of context, it seems to do that. One's pleasure is, however, a little dampened when one recalls that it comes from a speech put in the mouth of the Syracusan demagogue Athenagoras, for whom Thucydides obviously had no time at all; he saw in him a kind of Sicilian Cleon, and introduces him to the historical stage in words similar to those he has used to describe his Athenian counterpart ('he was principal leader of the democrats and at that present time most influential with the generality of the people').[6] If Athenagoras was *not* a sympathetic character, Alcibiades on the whole *was,* and what he says, although exaggerated to conform with the speaker's propensities, will have found an echo of assent in Thucydides as he set it down.

There can be no doubt that, whatever his views on the nature of power, Thucydides regarded it as a mistake for a state to vest that power in the *demos* at large. *Demokratia,* a word newly in currency in the fifth century, emphasises that the *kratos* lay with the *demos.* There was an imbalance of its distribution. Although the equality which democracy introduced was much praised and, as D. Kagan notes, 'Athenian literature is full of references to its virtues',[7] and although Thucydides himself draws attention to that basic principle not only by means of such men as Athenagoras but also through Pericles himself,[8] nevertheless *isokratia* was something which *Sparta* was credited with having championed.[9] Under democracy the upper classes and the bourgeoisie, to whom Thucydides himself belonged, could feel that some in the now time-honoured phrase were beginning to be more equal than others. The pendulum had swung too far.

To us, of course, the term democracy conveys that very idea of equality of duty, service, privilege, and justice which it conveyed to a conscientious Athenian democrat but failed to convey to Thucydides and his friends. We must however not forget that to them *'demos'* had two senses—a sense in which, as in an Athenian decree, it could mean the sovereign Athenian people as a whole, and a sense in which it could mean a political faction, the 'left wing', as we might

say. So that when the *demos* had *kratos,* it did not necessarily imply, without equivocation, that a completely
egalitarian society had been realised. It meant, on the interpretation of some, that 'the left' had taken over. To the
aristocrats this was almost to say that power was in the
hands of the mob, and the word *plethos* emphasises the
numerical aspect of this concept. The 'many', *hoi polloi,*
now controlled the state, and Thucydides was one of those
who saw with misgiving the era of the common man, the
tyranny of the plebs which in 424 B.C. Aristophanes bravely
parodied in his fiercely critical comedy *The Knights.*

Aristophanes there depicts Demos as a foolish and arbitrary old man, a harsh master of his slaves Nicias and
Demosthenes, but easily led by the nose by his favourite
politicians.[10] However, the poet was not being wholly just
to the qualities and good sense of the Athenians. Given the
character of power as we discussed it in the previous chapter, and granted that the possessor of it will be motivated
by self-interest in its exercise and retention, it was arguable
that the Athenian people in fact followed out with great
effectiveness the principles we have examined. That, at any
rate, is the line which that anonymous pamphleteer known
as 'The Old Oligarch' pursues in his treatise on the Athenian state written, most probably, early in the Peloponnesian
War. He uses all the phraseology and jargon of party politics
in the Athens of his time.[11] The people are the 'base ones',
the πονηροί, while the upper classes are the βέλτιστοι, the
'best people', in Roman terms the *optimates.* He writes in
effect, as M. F. McGregor has put it, 'I do not approve of
democracy, but, if you must have it, I admit that the Athenians make a fine job of it'.[12] But this is not Thucydides'

view. Thucydides did not approve of democracy, and he 'saw no strength of wisdom whatsoever' in the rabble. The only stage at which it appeared to him to shine in any virtuous light was in the period of Pericles' lifetime; but that was because of Pericles, and in despite of the nature it was subsequently shown to possess. Once the great man was gone, it stood condemned by its own inadequacies and by the verdict of historical facts.[13] We are in consequence led to consider what are the particular factors at work when we put the principles of power illustrated in Thucydides' history, which were considered in the first chapter, into relation with his views on democracy and his record of that democracy in power.

The possessor of *kratos* acquires from his possession a certain *dynamis*. Using the verb cognate to that noun, he δύναται, he 'can', he is *potens* in the Latin sense.[14] He has the capabilities, resources of strength and materials, all that is implied in words like the adjective δυνατός and others of the same root. Under the principles already investigated, the *demos,* thus equipped, will look to its security, under the influence of δέος, will act always with regard to its ultimate self-interest (ὠφελία), and will believe in, and seek to foster and defend, its dignity and honour (τιμή).[15] It may or may not temper its rule with justice (δικαιοσύνη); Thucydides implies his own judgement that it did not so temper its rule, but is honest enough to allow the probably more general Athenian view that it *did* to be given a hearing.[16] In fact, although Aristophanes depicts the *demos* as arbitrary, and in the Melian Dialogue Thucydides argues that the springs of its action are pretty close to those which Callicles and Thrasymachus would endorse, that particular interpretation of power is the interpretation least likely to be used by a popular government. For popular opinion, as we shall investigate in a later chapter, is more emotional and sentimental, diverted from a strict reckoning of policy on the basis of expediency by the intervention of what people consider to be humane and moral factors.[17] When in 427 B.C. the Athenians reversed their originally harsh decision to execute all the male citizens of Mytilene, which had revolted from them, they are rebuked by their own hero Cleon on this very score of over-great humanitarianism. A democracy cannot rule an empire in the way it should be ruled because the people are too sentimental, and are therefore weak and hesitant when a crisis demands they be strong and ruthless. 'The City', as Sir Frank Adcock put it,[18] 'embodies power, and power grows from power and nothing else. No other interests may prevail against it, no other criterion is in place. The ancient mythical past of Athens was full of stories of generosity and protection of the weak, but, in the present, exhibition of these qualities is limited by the immediate interests of the state. If moderation is politic, a means to create a more lasting power, it is a virtue, but only then.'

Both Cleon and Thucydides saw this; Cleon urged its application. Thucydides, though realising the force of such a principle and perhaps its inevitability as a concept, objected to it in practice. The people could not easily be persuaded to it. It is noteworthy that the whole argument in the Mytilenaean debate revolves round it, but it is not the point at issue for which the debate had been called.[19] The *demos* had not decided to reopen the issue of comparative expediency, but had repented of its earlier inhumanity. Cleon has to remind them of the real factors which should govern the

issue, and recalls the debate to its proper footing. His sentiments were well translated into a modern context when,
to the assembled convention in San Francisco which nom-
inated him a candidate for the Presidency of the United
States, with equal force, with equal sincerity, with equal
justification, and with equal truth, Barry Goldwater declared
'Extremism in the defence of liberty is no vice; moderation
in the pursuit of justice is no virtue'.[20] Liberal opinion pro-
fessed itself shocked and offended by so uncompromising
a declaration, but it invites reflection. If we do not find ourselves in agreement with Goldwater and with Cleon, we
must ask ourselves seriously why we do not. At what point
are we to abate our defence of liberty? At what stage do we
draw rein on our pursuit of justice? On what principle do
we make selection of that point or of that stage? These are
relevant problems no less at the present time than they were
in 427 B.C. They are equally at home in California as in
Attica. They insist on an answer from us in our circumstances as forcefully as they insisted on an answer from the
Athenians in theirs.

Thucydides' realisation of the demands and implications
of *dynamis* may be easily appreciated from the number of
times the word appears in his *History*—most particularly in
his first book, which is, after all, the explanatory book laying before us so much that is to be fundamental to the
interpretation of what is to come.[21] *Dynamis* is the hallmark
of the successful city-state, the *polis*. Mere *opsis,* looking at
a city, does not provide a sufficient index to it, Thucydides
says, as may be judged from the appearance of Mycenae and
Sparta.[22] The remains of Mycenae did not reflect the great
power once enjoyed by Agamemnon, and the physical

aspect of Sparta would, in his view, lead after-ages to the misconception that its importance cannot have been so considerable as in fact it was.[23] *Dynamis* is won in war, or by making the right friends. It can be dissipated by internal discord or blocked by external opposition. The Corinthians in their speech at Athens on the Corcyrean crisis claim that it is enhanced by restraint ('not wronging one's compeers') rather than by taking risks which superficially may seem attractive. Themistocles, we are told, saw that the acquisition of *dynamis* was the end towards which his policy, on his city's behalf, should be directed. The Athenians at Sparta are made by the historian to express their pride in it; they regard it as natural that they should seek to retain it once they had acquired it; they note that their exercise of it is more gentle than the laws of power entitle them, but imply that that entitlement is in itself unexceptionable.[24] Chapter 118 shows *dynamis* as the key to the Peloponnesian War, the successful accomplishment of what Themistocles had long ago envisaged. Significantly, perhaps, it is Pericles who in his last speech raises what is almost a paean to it[25]: 'Athens to-day possesses a power which is the greatest that ever existed down to our time.' 'What you think is that your dominion consists solely of your allies', he tells the Athenians; 'but', he continues, 'I have something else to tell you. The whole world before our eyes can be divided into two parts, the land and the sea. Of the whole of one of these parts you are in control—not only of the area at present in your power, but elsewhere too, if you want to go further. With your navy as it is to-day there is no power on earth, not the King of Persia nor any people under the sun— which can stop you from sailing where you wish. This power of yours is something in an entirely different category from all the advantages of houses or cultivated land' [which the Athenians who lived in the country had had the courage to abandon to Spartan depredation at the outbreak of war].²⁶ 'You may think that when you lose them you have suffered a great loss, but in fact you should not take things so hardly; you should weigh them in the balance with the realities of power and see that, in comparison, they are like flower-gardens and other elegances which are the ornament of wealth, not its substance.' The trouble with Thucydides was that he liked and enjoyed Athenian power and he endorsed this kind of expression of it, but that he would not or could not envisage the virtues of the *demokratia* which had produced it.

Athenian *dynamis* had created the Athenian *arche*. *Arche* (ἀρχή) expresses both the exercise of power once it has been obtained, and the sphere of that exercise, what in the case of Athens we customarily call 'the Athenian Empire', although in this day and age, when 'Empire' as a word in itself unfortunately and undeservedly conveys a pejorative meaning, some other translation should be found for a word which in its nature is essentially neutral. *Dynamis* leads to *arche* by a process of κρατεῖν. The superior strength expressed by this verb and employed in this process is *kratos,* and having successfully employed it you may be described by the superlative adjective κράτιστος. Now this last word so acquires a selection of shades of value-meanings that it can only be conveyed by a variety of Latin equivalents— *fortissimus* or *peritissimus* or *optimus,* according to your judgement of the situation.²⁷ All are the expression of refined ability. But whether a man is *fortis* or *peritus* or quite simply *bonus,* and if a city on a comparable basis of ability has been able to acquire *arche* and to become κράτιστος, there is always a danger. As we noted in the last chapter, whether it is deserved or undeserved, the result is to provoke envy and dislike (*phthonos* and *echthos*); for *arche* has to be exercised over others, and the others do not like it.[28] The active verb, ἄρχειν, is a fine thing, both in principle and specifically for the subject of the verb. In the passive it is obnoxious, and even worse when it is rubbed home: ἄρχεσθαι κατὰ κράτος ('to be ruled on a basis of force') expresses the unpleasant reality of the situation,[29] and is contrary to the τιμή, the honour, and ὠφελία, the advantage, of the ruled (οἱ ἀρχόμενοι). To suffer such a fate is their worst δέος, or dread, as Thucydides, at the beginning of the Peloponnesian War, loses no time in pointing out.[30] Therefore a combination of δέος and ὠφελία, fear and advantage, makes people try to fend off the possibility of τὸ ἄρχεσθαι, of being ruled.[31] For this involves the forfeiture of αὐτονομία, 'self-government', and therefore *arche* may be contrasted with the principle most dear to all Hellenic hearts, ἐλευθερία, 'freedom'.

It was observed in the previous chapter that of its nature power can never be static. There is that 'restless desire of Power after Power', which Hobbes posited as natural to mankind. It must expand or contract, and it is that law of expansion and contraction in general which underlies its application in particular (the expansion of Athens and the corresponding contraction of Sparta) to the causes of the Peloponnesian War. The *dynamis* of an expanding power is itself dynamic in effect and imparts dynamism; its function is that of a dynamo. For the Athenian people two events had set the dynamo working at full pressure; one was the establishment of the constitution of Cleisthenes which laid the foundations of fuller democratic development, and the other was the unexpected triumph over the Persians following the adoption of a policy of expanding Athens' naval potential.[32] Paradoxically, the success against Persia at first put on the brakes. Aristotle establishes two phases of the growth of popular power in his *Constitution of Athens,* one in the 480's and the other in the late 460's, when the 'full democracy' may be said to have been finally established, even though later decades brought improvements in detail. It is interesting to note the terms in which Aristotle expresses this growth: at one point he says 'the people were now more self-confident', and at another, 'the common people were waxing strong'.[33] Αὔξησις, 'growth', refers not to physical numbers but to strength of will and command, and such growth is linked with θάρσος, 'confidence'. Self-confidence, belief in themselves, based, as is frequently emphasised, on their participation in Athens' naval success, and belief in their democratic mission, was the key to the success of the Athenian people. They came to realise and to confide in their own power to achieve. The Corinthians, in their character sketch of them at Sparta, mingle *phthonos* with *echthos* in a sort of wry eulogy of their restless activity, as unsparing of themselves as it was of others. 'While you Spartans are hanging back, they never hesitate; while you stay at home, they are always abroad; for they think that the farther they go the more they will get. Of them alone it may be said that they possess a thing almost as soon as they have begun to desire it, so quickly with them does action follow upon decision. And so they go on working away in hardship and danger all the days of their lives, seldom enjoying their possessions because they are always adding to them. Their view of a holiday is to do what needs doing; they prefer hardship and activity to peace and quiet. In a word, they are by nature incapable either of living a quiet life themselves or of allowing anyone else to do so'.[34] We may take notice of the particular phrase that 'they are always adding to' what they have: τὸ αἰεὶ κτᾶσθαι. Such an expression, or its equivalent in other contexts, ὀρέγεσθαι or ἐφίεσθαι τοῦ πλέονος, aiming at or grasping after something more, recurs in the pages of Thucydides like a Wagnerian *leitmotiv*.[35] The noun to which such a verbal expression gives birth is πλεονεξία, which in Thucydides carries overtones of moral condemnation. It is not without interest that three of the four instances of its use in his pages occur in his discussion of the revolution in Corcyra.[36]

However, if πλεονεξία is to Thucydides the pursuit of more, the expansion of power, carried to excess, it was to the thoroughgoing democrat a virtue and to even the less thoroughgoing a natural phenomenon.[37] Both Callicles in Plato's *Gorgias* and Thrasymachus in the first book of the *Republic* believe it to be a characteristic of the good man (ἀγαθός), for the expression of democratic virtue was not only to establish *isonomia* and *demokratia* at home but to possess the capacity and will to rule over others successfully.[38] This latter virtue is one which our own world vehemently denies and rejects, and this makes it the more difficult for us to approach its affirmation in fifth-century democracy with any sympathy or understanding; but we must make the effort. The restless dynamism and urge to expansion involved, therefore, what may be described as 'multifarious activity'. The word they used for this (πολυπραγμοσύνη)[39] need mean no more than 'doing things', with the implication of 'many things', 'everywhere', and 'all the time'; but the translation which is generally preferred, 'meddlesomeness', gives it a more sinister implication. There is no reason why it should have that implication. It was a word only once used by Thucydides,[40] and there he makes the Athenians use it of themselves as a point in their favour. Their activity is imposed on them, they claim, as a form of self-defence. Δέος, that is to say, and ὠφελία make it necessary. 'We are forced to intervene in many directions simply because we have to be on our guard in many directions; in Hellas we rule in order not to be ruled.'[41] 'Make full use', they say to the men of Sicilian Camarina, 'of our interventionism and our general character, which fits in with your own interests'—and they reasonably judge that for the Camarinaeans the clinching argument ought to be what is in the best interests of Camarina. The Loeb translator, C. Forster Smith (it is not, however, his translation here quoted), feels it advisable to say in a footnote, that the verbal phrase 'πολλὰ πράσσειν, as well as the noun πολυπραγμοσύνη, is used in a good sense, characterising the policy of the Athenians at their acme, as described by Pericles in the Funeral Oration'.

To this point we shall return in a little while, in relation to Thucydides' view of Periclean democracy. For the moment we must add to this part of the argument Thucydides' opinion, reasonable enough on the face of it, that dynamic power ought to be exercised with *sophrosyne*: if it is, the victims of it are less liable to create disturbances and commit atrocities.[42] Now *sophrosyne* is not an easy word to represent.[48] It conveys the ideas of 'restraint' and 'moderation', of having a proper regard for the courtesies and niceties of life, of doing things in an orderly and decorous manner, 'comme il faut', and behaving like a respectable and responsible person. *Dynamis* tempered with it will thus be exercised in a sober and restrained manner, and will earn the respect of those who are the objects of it. In general terms this is all very well, but it is worth remarking that *sophrosyne* is most particularly an aristocratic virtue.[44] It is men undoubtedly of the 'right wing' whom Thucydides himself describes as *sophrones,* and the very description (since the word always carries a sense of approval, and is a 'good' word) reveals his endorsement of their point of view.[45] In his dialogue *Charmides,* which is concerned with the definition of *sophrosyne,* Plato sets it squarely in an upper-class context. If *arche* is exercised without it—and ill-educated possessors of *arche* are much in danger of this, since, as Plato argues it, they lack the essential knowledge without which no virtue can be understood and properly exercised—then there is a likelihood that the *dynamis* will produce a *tyrannis.* This *tyrannis* may be the tyranny of the individual, into whose hands an unsuspecting democracy may fall. Such a possibility, thanks to Dionysius of Syracuse, was more evident to Plato and Aristotle than to Thucydides. But the tyranny of an institution, more impersonal and therefore more unfeeling, was an even more serious proposition which Thucydides *did* recognise. For him the dictatorship of the proletariat was open *dynamis* untempered by any of the virtues of the better sort of people—those who called themselves the χρηστοί or βέλτιστοι or ἐπιεικέστατοι, 'the good people' or 'the best people' or 'men of sense and reason'. And ἐπιείκεια, 'equity', 'readiness to meet people halfway', is specifically rejected by Cleon as having any place in the policies of an imperial democracy.[46] The Athenians at Sparta even go so far as to claim that, when Athens *has* shown such readiness, her reward has been not credit but its reverse, ἀδοξία.[47] The world begins to despise a great power which does not live up to its capacities and exercise the *dynamis* it undoubtedly has.

What the people cannot do, in their enthusiastic πολυπραγμοσύνη, is to keep their heads, to exercise σωφροσύνη, and to distinguish what is best for them. Taken individually they have not the qualities to do it for themselves; and, even if some individuals were to be found with the requisite qualities, the effect of the people acting *en masse* would be to stifle the effective emergence of these minority virtues. The people at large can only depend on the advice they get, and if they are led by the nose, as Aristophanes describes, by those who lead them, their leaders at least must possess the requisite sobriety and judgement which will enable them to give a *good* lead. *Kratos,* that is to say, must be exercised with *sophrosyne* on the basis of *gnome.* Now *gnome* also tends to be an aristocratic quality, and is emphasised as such by Theognis as early as the mid-sixth century.[48] We may note that Themistocles, for whom Thucydides reserves his highest terms of praise, has all his great qualities summed up in the expression that he was κράτιστος γνώμων and endowed with a δύναμις φύσεως.[49] That is to say, that his ability to use his judgement was very powerful indeed, and that his whole character had a dynamic quality which inspired his every action. If power is used with judgement, it produces material success and prosperity. This has already, in Thucydides, been exemplified as the basis of Agamemnon's power:[50] being more powerful, δυνατώτεροι, and possessing *periousia,* he says, these maritime princes made the other cities subject to themselves. Περιουσία, or περιουσία χρημάτων, material affluence, is the product of power wisely used and itself enhances power. Wars are won, said Pericles, by a combination of *gnome* and *periousia:*[51] and, significantly returning to an important element to which I have already referred, he told the Athenians, since they possessed both these essentials, to 'be confident', θαρσεῖν.[52]

To sum up, then, as far as the argument has taken us, we are now in a position to say what were the characteristics or factors or qualities which had made the Athenian democracy great and had brought it success. They may be listed as *kratos, dynamis, tharsos, gnome,* and *periousia.* The first two are aspects of power itself, the next two are necessary concomitants of its successful use, and the last the product of power contributive to its further increase. The Athenians possessed all of them, and it was in virtue of them that they had triumphed.

But what was it in popular government that Thucydides criticised and mistrusted? This too we may analyse on the basis of the same list of these five qualities, and we have indeed already observed him making some of his principal points about them. In the first place he draws attention to the likely jeopardization of *kratos* through τοῦ πλέονος ὀρέγεσθαι, over-extension of aim and ambition.[53] This process is assisted by ἐλπίς, hope, and by ἔρως, desire,[54] and we may note that Plutarch later was to speak of the Athenian project of conquering Sicily as a δύσερως ἔρως, an 'ill-desired desire'.[55] Equally inimical to *kratos* is *stasis*, civil discord. The absence of *stasis* among the Spartans was a principal reason for their capability of exercising *dynamis*, their being δυνάμενοι.[56] John Finley correctly pointed to the contrast between Spartan stability and Athenian discord as fundamental to Thucydides' final judgement on the reasons for Athens' defeat.[57]

Secondly, Thucydides considers that *dynamis* had been misused: it had been exercised not with *sophrosyne* but with βία, force, and ὕβρις, arrogance, in keeping with a philosophy of power Thucydides' judgement on which we investigated in the preceding chapter. Lack of *metriotes*, moderation, had alienated friends and encouraged foes, and was dangerous, in consequence, to the city's well-being and safety, ἀσφάλεια.[58] Thirdly, the Athenian *demos*, and its leaders, in Thucydides' view, lacked the essential *gnome* without which it was almost inescapable that fatal blunders should be made. Thucydides makes this plain in his summing-up of the inadequacies, as he saw them, of the radical democracy in Chapter 65 of Book II, a passage cardinal in any study of the Athenian state and its alleged decline in the last quarter of the fifth century. Shortage of *gnome*, Diodotus tells us in the Mytilenaean debate, coupled with ἀπαιδευσία, lack of the proper mental equipment, go hand in hand with sheer folly (ἄνοια), with passion (ὀργή), and with precipitate rashness (τάχος).[59] In the fourth place we may set the net effect of the three previous evils—the dissipation of *periousia*. Reckless adventures, internal strife, expenditure on issues which would never have arisen but for democratic mismanagement—all these produced a situation in which the solid foundation of national wealth had been cut away, and the Athenians suddenly found their lack of *periousia* (and the Spartans' corresponding acquisition of it) as the most fatal of all fatal symptoms which in the end brought them to defeat. Lastly, the unhappy characteristics of the sovereign people, operating as a policy-making body, would not perhaps have been so fraught with bad consequences as they were, had it not been for the fifth element, that of confidence, θάρσος. We have seen that θάρσος had been the basis for the rise of democracy in the first place, and needed to be the basis for its successful continuance.[60] But, instead of maintaining itself at a steady and comfortable level, it oscillated. The Great Plague in the early part of the Archidamian War did it a great deal of damage; Brasidas' exploits in Thrace further affected it.[61] Pericles, as we have seen, knew when to foster it and knew that it had on occasions *to be* fostered.[62] The people's morale went up and down. They were encouraged by Pericles' last speech, and were, we are told, 'more zealous for the war'; but they continued their resentment against Pericles nevertheless, deposed him from his generalship and fined him. Soon afterwards, however, Thucydides observed, 'as is the way with the multitude', they re-elected him to his office.[63] Ἀλλοίωσις τῶν γνωμῶν, changes of mind or mutations of judgement on the basis of alternate optimism and pessimism, added to the instability of the state, and bouts of it are more than once characterised as a feature of 'the crowd'.[64]

What had made Pericles great, and Periclean democracy so much superior to what came after, was that under him all the virtues of democracy had been retained and allowed to flower, while the defects which we have just listed were kept under control. A democracy, to all intents and purposes, it certainly was; it operated as one, and exercised the power it had acquired.[65] But Thucydides, in one of his most famous phrases, contrasts theory and practice, appearance and reality. What Pericles did was to control the democracy, to restrain it from excess, and to exercise a moderating influence upon it. His doing so did not, on Thucydides' interpretation, infringe the essential ἐλευθερία, freedom, without which the *kratos* of the *demos* would have been wholly fictional. Though others referred to Pericles' 'tyranny' and called his companions latter-day Peisistratidae,[66] in an allusion to the Athenian tyrant of a century earlier, Thucydides counters such a charge almost *totidem verbis* with his phrase κατεῖχε τὸ πλῆθος ἐλευθέρως, 'Pericles restrained the multitude in a manner consistent with their freedom'.[67] Secondly, *kratos* was safeguarded because overextension of ambition, τοῦ πλέονος ὀρέγεσθαι, was in Thucydides' opinion avoided. This implied a proper use of Athenian *dynamis,* to which Thucydides, like Pericles, was far from taking exception. We have seen that *polypragmosyne* was a feature of Periclean democracy—the whole history of the Pentekontaetea is the record of it—if we use that word in its good sense. In its bad sense Pericles was against it, and feared its consequences if it were unchecked. Thucydides interpreted this as a defensive, unadventurous policy, but that is to misunderstand it, to stress its negative and not its positive quality. Plutarch perhaps expressed it with greater accuracy—'Pericles kept on checking their *polypragmosyne,* and diverted the greatest part of their *dynamis* to the task of safeguarding and strengthening what they already possessed.'[68] Thucydides expressed the same idea more negatively, in terms of what he calls ἡσυχία, which may mean 'peace and quiet' or even 'quietism'. But this had earlier been stigmatised by the Corinthians as a kind of conservative imperturbability peculiar to the Spartans, and absolutely uncharacteristic of Athens.[69] Thucydides' own predilections are apparent in its use, for we find that it is also the specific attribute of the *sophrones*. No, Pericles was by no means an opponent of *polypragmosyne* —quite the reverse in fact, for it was the inactive, uninvolved man, the ἀπράγμων, whom he rebuked.[70] You have your dominion, he reminded the Athenians, and you must get on with it, even if anybody 'in a mood of sudden panic and in a spirit of political apathy actually thinks that it would be a fine and noble thing to give it up'. Finally, that Pericles emerges constantly in Thucydides' account of him as possessing *gnome* to a marked degree and realising its value, as stressing *periousia,* and realising *its* value, and maintaining the *tharsos* of his fellow-citizens at the right level, not too little and not too much, I have already sufficiently suggested; turn the pages of the *History,* and the points will be illustrated readily enough.

The death of Pericles gave Thucydides the occasion to write his famous condemnation of the great man's political successors and to describe the decline of what, under Pericles, had been a successfully run democratic system. When he wrote that, the events in Sicily and afterwards were in his mind, for Chapter 65 of Book II is, on any account of the 'composition-problem' of the work, an addendum written when the full history of the war had unfolded itself. By 413 all the virtues of Periclean democracy had in Thucydides' view given way to their corresponding vices. We may find all the five points of *ḳratos, dynamis, gnome, periousia,* and *tharsos* as still cardinal, but in an inverted sense, to the exposition of the final book of the *History*. The very first chapter indeed sets it all out. When the news of the catastrophe in Sicily was brought to Athens, the Athenians looked round them and realised that they now had no ships, no men, and no money (i.e., they no longer possessed their essential *periousia*). What it all added up to, in fact, was a total loss of *ḳratos*. And this inevitably restricted, as a consequence, their exercise of *dynamis*. What is more, when this had happened, their enemies and former allies found them no longer an adversary to fear or a leader to respect, but an object of contempt. Thucydides speaks of the Chians, for instance, as 'despising the powerlessness of the Athenians'.[71] Not only was this (at least to some extent) the fruit of lack of *gnome,* but the subsequent history of the oligarchic revolution and the manner in which the *demos* was then hoodwinked emphasises that that lack of *gnome* was no passing phenomenon. It is seldom, in any case, that the word even appears in Book VIII. Last of all, as to *tharsos,* the opening chapter of the book goes on to describe the depression and despair with which the Athenians surveyed their gloomy prospects. 'In view of what had happened they were beset by fear and the greatest imaginable consternation'. Security, esteem, and self-interest, we recall, were the three objects of the exercise of power. With φόβος, fear, replacing the first, the other two were also at peril—τιμή, honour, so Phrynichus suggests to his colleagues,[72] besmirched by τὸ αἰσχρόν, disgrace, and the other, ὠφελία, self-interest or advantage, quite simply swallowed up in κίνδυνος, danger.

Are we to see real substance in the charges which Thucydides made about popular power, as exemplified in the Athenian experience? It is, I believe, not for us to judge, and certainly not for us to judge on our own standards of political morality, as the last chapter sought to emphasise. We should content ourselves with observing that the charges were made, and that the Athenians laid themselves open to them. Granted the premisses on which power and its exercise are to be based, the *demos* managed their *kratos* well; that is, at least, the view of their admiring and frustrated opponent the Old Oligarch,[73] and one which we can share with some confidence, for it is a view which we may well judge to be upheld by the facts as far as we can see them. That the Athenians lost the war does not invalidate the merits of their system, although Thucydides gives the impression of thinking that it does. It is a system they continued to follow, and it is a system in which we ourselves believe. Thucydides' view seems to be that such virtues as a system that it might have had were cancelled out by its inefficiency; centralisation of control and exercise of a superior *gnome* are to him indispensable. Our own view is, I suppose, that inefficiency is a reasonable price to pay;[74] the price in the past for a democracy has sometimes been that of failure in face of the effectiveness of a centralised military organisation or the cleverness of a single individual with his personal and therefore centralised *gnome*. That is why 'freedom perished at Chaeronea' in 338 and why Sparta, backed by Persia, triumphed in 404. But in accepting the shortcomings and hazards of a less efficient system we have come to find that, even taking these into account, *demokratia* properly organised has a *kratos* unrecognised by Thucydides. In its hour of need it may indeed find a κράτιστος γνώμων who may guide it and respect it, as the Athenians found Themistocles and Pericles and as the British found Winston Churchill. But in itself it possesses an inner strength which, against all reason and often against all logic, saves it in the end.

Aristophanes' portrayal of *Demos* as an old man has its parallel in a relief surmounting an Athenian decree of 336 B.C., in which a female figure, *Demokratia,* crowns with laurel a seated, bearded, elderly gentleman, *Demos.*[75] The image is a mistaken one. History has repeatedly demonstrated that when a democracy faces real crisis, the *Demos* has all the courage and resilience of a vigorous youth. In Athens' case, that youthful vigour is apparent in Thucydides' narrative, but Thucydides does not appear to recognise it. For ourselves we know it from our own history. The experience of Athens, where democracy for a brief time faltered, may have been unfortunate and untypical. *We* may judge, from our own experience and that of our immediate forebears, that the strength of *demokratia* is its solidarity in defence of its honour and its advantage, and its unanimity with regard to its apprehensions, when backs are to the wall. In the Athens of Thucydides, either the *stasis* to which the historian so emphatically pointed (if we accept his diagnosis as correct) prevented this inner strength from developing, or, present and yet unnoticed by him, it proved in the crisis insufficient. But as a factor it has shown itself, twice already in the twentieth century, so important an element in modern democracy as to belie the adverse judgement Thucydides saw fit to pass on that democracy's fifth-century prototype.

Chapter 3

It was their contention . . . that the number of those with a share in the government should be limited to five thousand, and that these should be the people best equipped to serve the state either in their own proper persons or with their resources.

Thucydides VIII 65, 3

Let us choose a certain number of the best men in the country, and set the power in their hands. It is only natural to suppose that the best men will produce the best policies.

Herodotus III 81
(reporting the advice of the Persian noble
Megabyzus to King Darius of Persia)

In contemplating revolutions, it is easy to perceive that they may arise from two distinct causes—the one to avoid or get rid of some great calamity, the other to obtain some great and positive good.

Thomas Paine, *The Rights of Man*

He that goeth about to persuade a multitude that they are not so well governed as they ought to be, shall never want attentive and favourable hearers.

R. Hooker, *Ecclesiastical Polity* I

Men are made by nature unequal. It is vain, therefore, to treat them as if they were equal.

J. A. Froude, *Party Politics*

Power and the Elite

THE last chapter dealt with power in the hands of the majority, power in the actual possession of a democracy, and with the nature and character of its exercise. This time we turn to the problems of a minority without power, an élite who thought of themselves as aristocrats and whose critics and enemies preferred to think of them as oligarchs. Because of the stimulus to acquisition which, as we have seen, is characteristic of power, it is not only natural that those who have it should seek to acquire more; it is natural also that those without it should seek to acquire it, and it is natural, further, that they should regard the obtaining of it not as a manifestation of ingrained ambition, of the *pleonexia* which we identified as inherent in mankind, but as the rectification of an injustice. Such an attempt at the acquisition of power forms one of the principal features of Thucydides' final book, when the changed circumstances of the Athenians, after the disaster in Sicily, had produced a crisis of confidence within the Athenian democracy. That the attempt was unsuccessful and comparatively short-lived in no way detracts from the value of a study of its motivation and execution.

In undertaking the study I recognise that the oligarchic movement of 411 B.C. has in general received from posterity what we should nowadays term 'a bad press'. This is to some degree enhanced by our inability to appreciate its inspiration—and I use the word 'appreciate' in its fundamental sense. Born and bred as we are in a democratic society, we are unlikely to commend the objectives of those who conspired to overthrow one. We are liable to find their methods as repugnant as their aims, and most of all we cannot profess, or would nowadays find it inexpedient to profess, any sympathy with their principles. But the historian cannot properly fulfil his function unless he is prepared, to the best of his ability, to enter into the circumstances with which he is dealing, to participate in the scene and, in the deepest significance of sympathy, to feel with those whose thoughts and actions he is examining. We must therefore be strict with ourselves in divesting ourselves of our ingrained or preconceived political attitudes, and in assessing what the Athenian oligarchs attempted to do with all the fellow-feeling for them that we can muster.

Our chief difficulty is that the idea that government should remain exclusively in the hands of those best qualified to govern is now at a discount. It is a logical concept that the art of administration demands certain qualities of mind just as the practice of medicine or any other skill. It is reasonable that a proper education in affairs, a good standard of knowledge and intelligence, alone can and should qualify a man to have a voice in the government of his country. Government based on ignorance, and votes prompted by irrationality and emotion, must on any unbiased analysis be ultimately harmful to a country's or a city's interests. Plato more than once attacks the folly of government carried on by the majority vote of ignorant amateurs. There is a famous passage on the subject from the *Protagoras,* and it may serve the present purpose to quote another, no less famous, from the *Gorgias*.[1] Socrates argues 'When the citizens meet to appoint medical officers or ship-builders or any other class of professional, surely it won't be the orator (i.e., politician) who advises them then. Obviously in every such election the choice ought to fall on the most expert. . . .and it is expert advice that will be called.' Gorgias argues that the orator's skill in speaking is so persuasive that it can outweigh the professional. But Socrates elicits a damaging admission from him—that the persuasion will be effective only before a popular audience. 'So when the orator is more convincing than the doctor', says Socrates, 'what happens is that an ignorant person is more convincing than the expert before an equally ignorant audience.'

On this basis Plato would, without doubt, condemn the British and American systems wholeheartedly. Because we cannot govern by means of a sovereign assembly of all the citizens meeting in one place, we have to delegate the authority to govern to our representatives—to people, what is more, who *want* to represent us and to govern. Now voluntarily to place power in the hands of those who actively seek it, and who flatter and cajole us in order to get it, is to Plato supreme folly. According to him, only those should be trusted to rule who do *not* want to do so, and who have to be compelled against their will to undertake the task.[2] What is more, in electing our representatives we also act on the principle, which we have elevated into a graven image before which all good democrats must bow, that every man should have an equal voice and an equal vote—as if all men had an equal capacity to judge the rights and wrongs of the situation, the needs of the country, the qualities of the candidate, and so forth, and as though all had an equal stake in the result. 'We hold these truths to be self-evident', begins the American Declaration of Independence, 'that all men are created equal . . .'. Thomas Jefferson, whose thought lies behind these words, has much to answer for to posterity. The sentiments of Froude, whose words are included among the quotations which preface this chapter, accord better with the facts. What is more, those with greater capacities and better understanding customarily fulfil in society positions of greater responsibility and are expected to assume greater burdens. Yet their voice in government is not commensurate with their responsibilities any more than it is commensurate with their merits; and although they deserve greater privileges in life because of their greater burdens, the very word 'privilege' is denounced as a symbol of inequality, nay of immorality, in a democratic context. The idea that a man should be suitably rewarded for his exertions, whether financially or in status or both, is overwhelmed, despite its essential logic, by the irrationality of an egalitarianism itself based on a false premiss.

In all this, therefore, we must not allow our modern prejudices to hamper our historical understanding. I must ask the reader, whatever his or her own principles may be, to envisage that the attitude to power I have just stated is a reasonable one, and to appreciate that people act, and have acted, on it in sincerity and good faith. It is an attitude that would have been shared—that *was* shared—wholeheartedly by many Athenians of the fifth and fourth centuries whose intellects we are taught to admire and many of whose judgements we have no hesitation in accepting. I have already referred to Plato; it would be easy to add by way of example Xenophon, Antiphon, Thucydides himself, and, if one looks outside Athens, to throw in Aristotle for good measure.

Government by the few may be an aristocracy of birth, of wealth, or of attainment (i.e., merit). As history unfolds, the aristocracy of birth is seen to be the ultimate end of all aristocracies, but the wise aristocracy always allows its ranks to be replenished by the wealthy and the meritorious, and those which have not done so have suffered. By arousing the hopes of those who seek to qualify to join it, such an aristocracy disarms the opposition of its cleverest and most dangerous opponents, and it averts its own stagnation by enlisting those who can help it most with the fresh vigour of their capital of brains or substance—their σώματα or their χρήματα. To survive, it must be liberal—it must be composed of 'the best people'. Overemphasis on material qualifications leads to plutocracy, overemphasis on exclusiveness leads to oligarchy. Both are corruptions of the ideal, as Plato shows in the *Republic* and the *Politicus,* though in corruption both rank as lesser evils than democracy.[3] But the hereditary principle seems to me ultimately inescapable and is on the whole not a bad index, in its results, of the success of an aristocracy at recruiting itself. The dynastic mentality is part of human nature; the family is the basic unit of society and its ties have a deep-seated force in our thinking. The wish to hand on what one has achieved—wealth, power, status, prosperity, education—to one's children is absolutely fundamental. It has baffled and will continue to baffle every attempt by social and religious reformers to override it. Such success as they may have in practice, as for example in Russia or China—or even in the Western world

—will be no more than temporary; a generation or two will see the old pattern re-established. 'And the brother shall deliver up the brother to death', said Our Lord in St. Matthew's Gospel,[4] 'and the father the child, and the children shall rise up against their parents and cause them to be put to death; and ye shall be hated of all men for my name's sake.' Revolutionary fervour does indeed cause these things to happen; but, once the fires have died down, the hereditary principle re-asserts itself, and society rests securely once more upon its proper foundations.

In the end, because of that principle, men will claim a right to power because they are the sons of their fathers. It is a fair presumption that, just because they are, they will be likely to have acquired in the course of their development more understanding of government than most.[5] Their milieu, from childhood up, will have been that of the possession and exercise of power, and their claim has reason behind it. Aristocracies usually have a particular code of conduct which regulates their dealings with one another and with their inferiors. The Greeks called it *kalokagathia;* for us it would amount to 'conduct becoming an officer and a gentleman'. It provided a sound basis of practical morality for everyday affairs, and it will receive further notice in the last chapter of this book. *What* it is, we may find more fully explained by Xenophon in his work on the Education of Cyrus. It met the problem of 'class' by accepting and then ignoring the existence of such a thing. Class consciousness is after all a phenomenon most particularly cherished by the lower orders. 'His lordship may compel us to be equal upstairs', said Crichton, that most admirable of butlers in Barrie's play, 'but there will never be equality in the servants' hall'.[6] Where a society is framed to be egalitarian, as was that of Puritan Massachusetts, class distinction is invented—and was there invented to such effect that Boston has become proverbial for it.[7] Near the end of *The Pirates of Penzance* it is revealed that the pirates are 'all noblemen gone wrong'. Their shortcomings are immediately forgiven. 'No Englishman unmoved that statement hears: because, with all our faults, we love our House of Peers'.[8] Gilbert's sentiment is not confined to England or to the nineteenth century. All the same, as we have seen, *phthonos* and *echthos* always pursue those who have power, and in the case of a minority in power the assault concentrates on 'privilege' and on a demand for equality, ἰσότης. The natural aristocrat accepts privilege and inequality as natural things. He finds opposition to them scarcely credible on grounds of principle, and interprets it correctly as the expression of self-interest it really is. Of the three aims of power which have been in our minds, security, status, and personal or sectional advantage, it may be presumed that an aristocracy is mindful of the first only when it is threatened, accepts the second as its natural due and, like all men, pursues the third. A βέλτιστος, one of the 'best' people, is not apt to be militant about the fact that that is what he is. His qualities and his claims speak for themselves, and that is that.

For the Athenian aristocrats, most of these general statements will fit well enough. At least, they will have been inherent in their attitudes and will have underlain their approach to the world they lived in. The trouble was that the *beltistoi* of Athens had fallen on evil times. They had a tradition, although the reality was long since past, that once they had controlled Attica, that once the λαός, the commons, had hearkened to their nobility, their βασιλῆες. They used to govern, and they ought to be governing now. But power now lay with the common multitude, the πλῆθος, not with the ὀλίγοι, the few, with whom it rightfully should lie. In the previous centuries of Greek history, the aristocrats' power had been usurped by tyrannical individuals—often one of themselves (as had happened both in Athens and elsewhere) who had been a renegade among his peers. Already in the mid-sixth century, the heyday of archaic Hellas, Theognis is lamenting the unhappy lot of the 'good men' oppressed by the bad and the wicked.[9] In Athens in more recent times they had, as it were, jumped from the frying pan into the fire. No sooner had the tyrant-house been expelled than democracy had begun to develop; and this was the more galling because the first steps down the slippery slope had been taken by one of themselves as part of an inter-aristocratic faction struggle for power. It was Cleisthenes the Alcmaeonid who had sold the pass; although we must with justice acknowledge that the development was the fault of them all—that having regained their Paradise Lost they fell to squabbling over it. So now it was the *demos,* the lower orders Cleisthenes had once thought to use, whom they saw enjoying the inheritance that was really theirs. Suspected and watched for what they had once been and for what they might again become, the Athenian aristocrats were powerless and were yet still envied and harassed. The upper class might take refuge in philosophy and the arts, in the palaestra, in such hereditary honours (for instance, in certain religious cults) as they still possessed, but to men of their intellect and qualifications this hardly sufficed. They must wait for—perhaps, if they could, they might even hasten—the day when they should come into their own.

Why could such a day not, as it seemed, dawn for them? What held it back? As they surveyed the Greek scene, they might well feel aggrieved that in no other city but their own was a radical democracy in charge. In Corinth, in Sparta, in Boeotia, in Thessaly, the right sort of persons ruled the cities in the right sort of way. In one or two places where there was democracy of a kind—Elis, Sicyon, Argos —it was less rabid than the Athenian version, so far as may be judged. Why had Athens to be the exception and they, the rightful guardians of the destiny of the greatest city of Greece, left in the cold? It was this sort of question, asked with a similar urgency and frustration, which the 'Old Oligarch', as he is generally called, tried to answer in the early years of the Peloponnesian War. His work, unique of its kind, has been transmitted, by a fortunate quirk of fate, among the lesser writings of Xenophon, but that it is not by Xenophon has long ago been universally acknowledged. Its title, *The Constitution of the Athenians,* is in its way a misnomer. It is not an historical description of the Athenian state and its machinery, but a partisan political pamphlet, the careful reading of which is essential background for any understanding of the oligarchic position and for an appreciation of the revolution which Thucydides describes in his eighth book. For in the 'Old Oligarch' we have the reflection of the sentiments and ambitions which produced that revolution. Why he is referred to as an *Old* Oligarch I can never understand. He is very much the angry young man; his youthful blood runs hot, and he is passionate and vehement with the convictions of a youthful idealism—for we must allow that idealistic passions may burn in all their purity on the right wing as well as on the left.

It has been much discussed when he wrote, and for whom. This is not in itself a discussion relevant to this context, and I need only restate my own belief on the first point that he was writing early in the Archidamian War, during the period when the Athenian democracy was at its zenith. Perhaps this very statement involves an answer to the second point. It may be that he was trying to explain to his friends abroad why he and his party could not intervene and put a stop to the senseless conflict which the mutual intransigeance of the two great power blocs had let loose upon the Greek world.[10] Possibly he was trying to explain as much to himself as well, to account for his own frustration and powerlessness. For his principal point, as has been emphasised in an earlier connexion, is that the *demos* manages its affairs well—in its own interests, of course[11]—and has a strength which precludes any such attempt to overthrow it. Having acquired power, it handles it effectively and efficiently, and true merit is excluded successfully from the reckoning. The common man knows on which side his bread is buttered, and organises his *polis* accordingly. In all fairness the Old Oligarch is prepared to hand him so much credit. The trouble is that the common man is so terribly common. It is not only that the *demos* controls what the aristocrats ought to control; they make it cheap and sordid in the process.[12]

For if there is one particularly striking feature about the Old Oligarch's pamphlet, it is the bitterness of his tone. We may smile a little at the transparent naïveté of his technical political terms. The upper classes are not only excellent in character (χρηστοί) and the best people (βέλτιστοι); they are also strong and steadfast (ἰσχυροί), men of capacity (δυνάμενοι), clever and skilful (δεξιώτατοι)—to name only a selection. These are all value-words, political jargon though they have become, and the Old Oligarch intends them as such. And we should bear in mind that Aristotle in his *Constitution of Athens* uses no fewer than five comparable value-words to represent the same people in the same sort of tone.[13] It is a choice of language that springs from the heart, and which speaks (and is meant to speak) to it. These were the people who were once the defence of the state, who as ἀγαθοί, men of the highest calibre, on horseback or in the hoplite line of battle earned thereby their right to rule.[14] Now that the defence of the state depended more upon the *nautikos ochlos*—the mob that provided the crews for the ships—even that chance of justifying their position was denied them. Small wonder that they were fundamentally and bitterly hostile to democracy. 'All over the world the best elements are opposed to popular power', our friend remarks,[15] and the sentiment is echoed by Alcibiades when, in exile, he sent word to those whom Thucydides describes as the 'best people' to say that he was prepared to come home on condition of being invited by a government of the few and not by the worthless rabble which had thrown him out.[16] To Aristotle, no lover of democracy, the democrats are *demos*, 'people', and *plethos,* 'multitude'. The Old Oligarch is not satisfied with such colourless phraseology. 'Base' or 'worthless' people, 'lunatics', the 'worst element', or the 'vilest of the citizen-

body'—those are the terms that suit them better.[17] He is like
the Southerner who never really understood that 'Goddam'
and 'Yankee' are two words. The riff-raff look like slaves,
and in the topsy-turvy Athenian scene slaves look like citizens. You might cuff one and then find yourself in court on
the charge of assault,[18] not only because you could not tell
the difference between an Athenian citizen and a slave, but
also because the absurd egalitarianism of Athens protected
slave as well as free man.[19] The philosophy of the democrat
revolves entirely around what is to his personal profit. He
is sunk in *kakonomia* and *amathia,* both at once—in a combination of bad laws and a state of ignorance; but apparently he enjoys it.[20] Such a situation, fulminates the Old
Oligarch, is in itself thoroughly bad, and for men like him
completely intolerable. Let those govern who know how.
Among the best people, the *beltistoi,* you will find precious
little *akolasia*—'excess', or 'inability to show restraint', and
precious little *adikia,* 'lack of justice or fair play'. Instead,
you will find an abundance of ἀκρίβεια εἰς τὰ χρηστά—
careful regard for all that is best and worthwhile. The
abundance to be found in the *demos,* on the contrary, is an
abundance of foolishness, disorder, and low behaviour
(ἀμαθία, ἀταξία, and πονηρία),[21] and this folly or ignorance coupled with poverty (πενία) and lack of education
(ἀπαιδευσία) propels them not towards what is best and
worthwhile but towards its very opposite—ἐπὶ τὰ αἰσχρά.
How can a man with such attributes presume to get up in
the assembly, as he does, and help to frame government
policy? How can such a man judge what is good for the
city? It is a sad fact, the Old Oligarch has to acknowledge,
that the *demos* would rather find in their fellow-citizens

εὔνοια, 'goodwill', towards themselves and their class, coupled though it be with ignorance and worthlessness, than to find ill-will towards their class from a governing aristocracy, even though it be endowed with wisdom (σοφία) and excellence (ἀρετή).²²

Here is an oligarchic champion, therefore, worked up into an extreme state of tension and frustration. His argument has a scarcely veiled undertone of desperation; it winds in and out as one furious thought after another imposes itself on him; his blood boils with rage and impatience as he reflects on the government to which he must perforce bow his head. Instead of κακονομία, a state where the laws are bad, he wants εὐνομία, a state where they are good, and this is a word which has now become part of the oligarchic vocabulary: but it is the very fact that there is no εὐνομία that keeps the *demos* in ἰσχύς, strength, and ἐλευθερία, freedom.²³ One day—*der Tag*—you will see the good men making laws; they will punish the πονηροί, the worthless ones, and shut the gates of the council and the assembly against them. So that from the pinnacle of their fortunes the *demos* will very quickly fall into a state of subordination, δουλεία, which is of course where they belong.²⁴

How had a man like this come to such a pass? Revenge is in his mind; it is more than the sharp exchange of partisan politics, more than a rather blimpish unwillingness to move with the times. *Stasis* presents itself to him as the only way out; he looks to military support from outside. He is, in Dryden's words, 'resolved to ruin or to rule the state'. He is oligarch first and patriot afterwards; or rather, he would feel it his greater patriotic duty to overthrow the democrats than to defeat the Spartans, who after all would not be at war had the militant Athenian democracy not compelled them into it. There had been a time when the ties of friendship between the best people in Sparta and Athens had kept Hellas in prosperity and peace, a dualism which the new democracy had disrupted. Indeed, common sentiment between the upper classes of different cities had an influence which tended to outweigh the common sentiment shared by all classes in their joint citizenship of a single *polis*. The same was true of the democrats also, as Diodotus explains in the Mytilenaean debate and as has been well expounded by de Ste Croix.[25] In our reading of Book VIII, therefore, it is this sort of thinking, honestly thought and conceived with burning conviction, that we must have in our mind. It is easy to condemn the oligarchs of 411 for failure and treachery. It is not so easy to appreciate that they did what they did because they were honestly convinced that they had to do it; and their actions would, in their eyes at least, amply merit the comment that they were aimed towards what is best and worthwhile and conceived in excellence.

The Old Oligarch is the product of a generation and more of humiliation. When, as Herodotus tells us, Cleisthenes took the *demos* into his political club, it was all over with the sort of political organisation which the ἑταιρεῖαι, the aristocratic societies, represented. They continued to exist, but the city was, so to speak, no longer run from their smoke-filled back rooms. The lead of Cleisthenes was plainly followed by many of his class, and at first was innocuous enough—a government of the bourgeoisie, rid of the dangers and excesses of a close oligarchy. The watchword was ἰσονομία, equality in the application of the law, for which *demokratia* became synonymous even though it hardly deserved to do so.[26] Such a government contented the moderates, the 'centre'; it continued to look to the hereditary leaders of opinion for its political spokesmen. The Alcmaeonids, the Philaids, Themistocles, Aristides, all were men of family. The bulk of traditional, conservative opinion went along with the new deal. Later ages could speak, not without justice, of the *aristokratia* of the Cleisthenic constitution.[27] Cleitophon, speaking in the assembly of 411 which set a body of commissioners at work to re-examine the constitution, urged that they take into account the laws of Cleisthenes as being closer to those of Solon than to the radical democracy of his own time.[28] After 462 much changed. The bulk of moderate opinion presumably still went along with the new democracy, especially when Pericles showed himself so inspiring and sensible a leader. These were the people to whom Thucydides, the historian, belonged. For him the evils of democracy, as we have seen, were kept in check so long as the great man lived. But others were less easily reconciled. As the pendulum swung more and more to the left, so the number increased of those who began to be dissatisfied with the way the Athenian political system was developing. To Thucydides Pericles may have been the last of the great statesmen; to others (and the tradition survives in our literature) he was the first of the demagogues. After 462, men like Aristides and Cimon were out of date. Their last successor, Thucydides son of Melesias, did his best to carry on their tradition and earns Aristotle's explicit commendation, but in the inevitable trial of strength with Pericles he was exiled for his pains.[29] Others—men like Nicias perhaps—served the state as best they might, accepting with grumbles what they could not change, under the general impulse of 'my city, right or wrong'. Those whom Thucydides the historian refers to as οἱ σώφρονες, the men of sense and moderation, had to look on and see, with what patience they could muster, everything going to the dogs. They had their votes, but, heavily outnumbered in the assembly, these would have only a negligible effect. Indeed, overt opposition to the *demos* and its sectional interests served only to identify its author and render him suspect. But these 'moderates' were not militant. This was left to the extreme right wing, the 'oligarchs' proper. At the time of the battle of Tanagra in 458 they had apparently tried, and failed, to enlist Spartan help in overthrowing the new constitution.[30] Since then, as the Old Oligarch has told us, the success of the democratic régime had made any further such attempt futile. But one day the chance would come. He could not see how or when, but he looked forward to it all the same.

How would it come? It could only come at some moment when the *demos* faltered and hesitated, when for once democratic confidence, τὸ θάρσος, wilted; and when that time came they could make capital out of it. There had been such a moment at the time of the mutilation of the Hermae in 415; at least, the moment was revealing in that it showed how nervous and jumpy the *demos* might become when strange things were afoot. 'Courage is the thing', said J. M. Barrie; 'all goes if courage goes'.[31] But the *demos* was well entrenched. Even after the catastrophe at Syracuse, an oligarchic coup d'état was out of the question—even if the oligarchs were themselves ready for one. There was no *stasis* or sudden movement; in spite of depression and despair the people showed sobriety and discipline, as Thucydides emphasises. It was an atmosphere of 'backs to the wall', and in the face of such determination and solidarity the right wing could not risk open opposition or muster the necessary accession of support which alone could give them the preponderance they needed.

But the Sicilian disaster had, as it were, pushed the door ajar, and the right moment was evidently near. The oligarchs still lacked *kratos* and therefore *dynamis*. But they did have *tharsos,* and they did have *gnome*. What is more, they also had a leader. What they proceeded to do provides a classic lesson in the art of seizing power—which, properly applied, is the art not of seizing it but of persuading those who have it to surrender it, for this is the surest way of acquiring it with a solid basis. This volume has no intention of appearing as a manual of revolution, nor is it part of the function of the Martin lecturer to offer advice on the best recipe for overthrowing a lawfully constituted government. But I think we may in this context properly investigate what are some of the essentials one must look to if one wishes to do that sort of thing. Thucydides, while not expounding them as such, allows them to appear clearly enough; they were, after all, inherent in the situation he was describing.

First, as I have already said, the occasion must be right. There is no point in raising revolutions that are doomed to failure from the start because the opposition is too strong. In 413 the moment was not quite right; in 411 it was. Why was that so? The answer to the question introduces the second necessary ingredient—accession of popular sympathy. Although the Athenians had rallied well after the Sicilian disaster, there was a strong current of opinion among the more moderate, centre group that all was not as it should be—that there must be something wrong with a system that could perpetrate so gigantic a failure as this. For the first time these people begin to emerge as a coherent body. They did not want to finish with democracy and return to oligarchy; all they wanted was some sort of safeguard which should prevent the democracy from rashness and extremism—'a democracy but not the same sort', they said, μὴ τὸν αὐτὸν τρόπον δημοκρατεῖσθαι. This was the 'party of Theramenes'[32]—oligarchic enough to press for, and later to secure, a restriction of the franchise to 5000 of the upper-class citizens.[33] Another product of the speculation about reform was the discussion and production of paper programmes and theoretical constitutions of which chapters 30–31 of Aristotle's *Constitution of Athens* preserve the echo.[34] In these circumstances oligarchic plans could go ahead, and the moderates could be accommodated in them. In fact, the moderate programme could be used for its wider appeal; once it had served its turn it could be discarded: 'This constitution of the 5000', said Thucydides, 'was only a piece of propaganda designed for the general public, since it was the revolutionaries themselves who were going to take over power in the city'.[35] The oligarchs knew the truth that Edmund Burke was later to enunciate, that 'the people never give up their liberties but under some delusion'.[36]

The third important thing is to encourage nervousness among the opposition and, if possible, to make its members mistrust one another. By such means it is possible to make the conspiracy seem larger and more comprehensive and more terrible, and so plans can take shape with greater freedom of manoeuvre. Again, Thucydides explains it in the clearest terms. 'The people kept quiet, and were in such a state of terror that they thought themselves lucky to be unmolested even if they had said nothing at all. They imagined that the revolutionary party was bigger than it actually was, and they lost all confidence in themselves. It was impossible for anyone who felt himself ill-treated to complain of it to someone else. In so large a city he would either have to speak to someone he did not know or someone he could not rely on. Throughout the democratic party, people approached one another with suspicion, everyone thinking that the next man had something to do with what was going on.'[37]

How could all this be brought about? Surely by the fourth and fifth ingredients of the successful revolution. The fourth ingredient is to have good, innocent-looking 'front men', in whom the mass of people might have confidence but who can afterwards be discarded if necessary, or who may indeed have, unbeknown to their former associates, revolutionary convictions of a genuine kind. Such a man was Peisander, who had once been a democratic leader, but who had by now come to believe in the revolution; but he was not alone—there were others.[38] Thucydides once more explains it to us. 'There were in fact among the revolutionaries some people whom no one would ever have imagined would have joined in an oligarchy. It was these who were mainly responsible for making the general mass of people so mistrustful of one another and who were of the greatest help in keeping the minority safe, since they made mutual suspicion an established thing in the popular assemblies'.[39] And the fifth ingredient? A judicious use of terrorism—the elimination of a few obnoxious irreconcileables, now here, now there; a man like Androcles the popular leader, for instance, who had been foremost in getting Alcibiades exiled. 'And some others that were inconvenient', says Thucydides,[40] 'they also made away with secretly, in the same manner'. The softening-up process then becomes cumulatively effective.[41] 'The people still convened in the assembly; but they discussed nothing that was not approved by the conspirators; not only were the speakers from this party, but what was to be said had been previously considered by them. No one dared to speak in opposition to them, through fear and because it was evident that the conspiracy was widespread. If anyone did oppose, at once and in some convenient way he was a dead man. And no search was made for those who had eliminated him, nor any action taken against those who were suspected of the deed'.[42]

Of course, the revolutionary programme, as I have emphasised, must not appear as such. I have already stressed the need for capitalising on a trend for change which is independently apparent, and for the use of good 'front men' to give the projected alteration in the balance of power a respectable appeal. It is also necessary to get the language right. This Thucydides explains elsewhere. 'What used to be described as a thoughtless act of aggression was now regarded as the courage one would expect to find in a party member; any idea of moderation was regarded as an attempt to disguise one's innate cowardice; ability to look at a question from all sides meant that a man was unfitted for action. Fanatical enthusiasm was the mark of the real man; to plot against an enemy behind his back was described as 'legitimate self-defence'. Anyone who held an extreme opinion was trustworthy, anyone who spoke against it was suspect. They used catchwords like 'equality for the masses within the constitution' (ἰσονομία πολιτική) and 'moderate aristocracy' (ἀριστοκρατία σώφρων), but in professing to serve the public interest they were bent on obtaining the prizes for themselves.'[43]

This was the sixth requirement. But to bring all these six into co-ordinated operation, to make everything work out with the necessary precision, you need the seventh and eighth requirements, plans and planners. You need to organise, and in the background you must have good organisation men. You need clever men who appreciate with Dryden that

> Plots, true or false, are necessary things
> To raise up commonwealths and ruin kings.[44]

When the day came and all was prepared, the commissioners who had been appointed to examine the constitutional question simply proposed that any motion should be accepted, i.e., that the normal procedure for blocking illegal proposals which might alter the democratic constitution should be abrogated. Whereupon Peisander moved the adoption of an oligarchic form of government, the details of which he outlined. No one expressed any opposition, and the job was done.[45] 'Conducted as it was by many able men', observes Thucydides, 'it is not surprising that the plot should have succeeded; for all that, it was an arduous task, for it was by no means easy, after the passage of almost a century since the tyrants had been overthrown, to deprive the Athenian people of their liberty'.[46]

What happened when the oligarchs were in power, and how and why they failed, it is not part of my purpose to describe. Any narrative must be largely based on the account that Thucydides gives,[47] and it is better to read him at first hand, since to retell his story can only diminish the impact of his superb description. What I have tried to do is to contribute to the better understanding of the Athenian élite and their attitude to power, and to appreciate the reasons for, and the methods employed in, their attempt to acquire it. We ought not to forget how Thucydides praises them as individuals, and in particular we must bear in mind what glowing terms he uses for his description of their gifted leader, Antiphon—'In quality of character he stood out above his contemporaries, and was exceptionally talented both in formulating ideas and in expounding them to others'.[48] These words are not lightly spoken by the historian. Here was a man for whom his admiration was great, and whom, he implies, we should be prepared to regard in similar terms. If our own political predilections cannot allow us to approve of what he stood for, we must acknowledge his right to stand for it, and we cannot but applaud the virtues of principle, thought, and action which he brought to the championship of his right.

It is the usual pattern in the textbooks to pass over the régime of the Four Hundred oligarchs at Athens with a description of what they did, coupled with implicit or explicit expressions of condemnation or, at the least, distaste. I suppose that this is the right thing to do. At any rate it is the politic thing to do. But my own inclination, which I would ask my readers to share, is to be sorry for them. They did what they thought right, on their analysis of the right, and they did it well. And it all came to pieces in their hands. 'Show my head to the people', cried Danton on the scaffold; 'it is worth it'. Antiphon, condemned by the restored democracy, would have been justified in saying the same. 'Show my head to the people'. This chapter has indeed sought, in a sense, to hold aloft Antiphon's severed head. It has done so in the belief that Antiphon *was*, as much as any man of his generation, worth it.

Chapter 4

For an individual autocrat or a city exercising imperial power nothing is contrary to good sense when it is conducive to self-interest.

Thucydides VI 85, 1

It is far from clear what was the attitude of Alcibiades himself towards the acquisition of autocratic power.

Plutarch, *Life of Alcibiades* 35

A city accustomed to freedom can be more easily ruled through its own citizens, if you want to keep it under control, than in any other way.

Machiavelli, *Il Principe* 5

Nature hath left this tincture in the blood
That all men would be tyrants if they could.

Daniel Defoe

Power and the Individual

O<small>N</small> the very eve of the great Athenian expedition to Syracuse, when the fleet was prepared, the generals furnished with the necessary means, and the troops ready to embark, the statues of Hermes, which by custom stood at doorways and in sacred places in the city, were mutilated during one single night in a widespread and evidently systematic operation. In the course of his sixth book, Thucydides several times reverts to the agitated state of mind induced in the Athenian *demos* as a result of this sacrilege and as a result also of the profanation of the Mysteries which the investigation of the mutilation uncovered. This agitation, which revealed itself in the assembly and among the demagogues, was exploited by the oligarchs; at least, this is the opinion of Malcolm McGregor,[1] and in view of the considerations advanced in the last chapter it is evident that it has much to be said for it. But the ugly temper and the suspicions of the people were directed not only towards a possible oligarchic coup.[2] The alternative which they feared was a conspiracy designed to set up a tyranny, and it is to this alternative that we ourselves must now turn. How does the *individual* in search of power fit into the concept of power which we have been discussing, and how does fifth-century Athenian democracy, with *its* concepts of power, suit him? Tyranny, the Athenians remembered, had in their own case ended by being oppressive, and had been overthrown not by Harmodius and Aristogeiton, as a popular fallacy liked to suppose,[3] but by Spartan intervention. The possibility of its recurrence as much as a century later put them in such consternation that we may realise the impression the whole concept, and prospect, of the autocracy of an individual had upon them. They abhorred it in theory and they had rejected it in practice. Yet it presented itself to them as an evident and constant danger, and in a crisis they were ready to see a conspiracy in its support lurking round every corner.

Even so, no fear of a revived tyranny could strike very deep were there not a potential candidate to fulfil the role of tyrant. The idea of the loss of liberty at the hands of a dictator would of course be regarded as anathema at any time; but only the advent of a likely autocrat would convert theoretical worries into real and serious ones. The trouble was that in 415 there was such a candidate in their midst, Alcibiades, and this is made explicit by Thucydides early in Book VI.[4] Consequently our study of power and the individual in this context must be the study of power and Alcibiades. It is a pleasure to make the conversion. For Alcibiades exercises as great a fascination now, at more than 2300 years' distance, as he did then. He remains a controversial figure, an irresistible and completely charming enigma. He puzzles us still, but we cannot lay the puzzle aside, and for any interpretation of the last two decades of the fifth century we must not. Nor could Athens. At the very end of the war, when everything was all but lost, it remained the ultimate, all-important question which Dionysus put to Aeschylus and Euripides in his adjudication of their contest in Aristophanes' *Frogs,* and which the

Athenians in general doubtless put to one another—'how far can we trust Alcibiades?'[5]

It is remarkable that the reverse of the question—'how far could Alcibiades trust the Athenians?'—has never been adequately considered. Yet this form of the question is a relevant one in respect of any man in search of political power, and in the case of Alcibiades it becomes particularly relevant if we look at the situation, as we should, from Alcibiades' personal point of view. Thucydides may reflect Alcibiades' own opinion when he regards the failure of the Sicilian Expedition not as brought about through an error of original planning but as caused by the people's lack of trust in Alcibiades personally.[6] His various remarks about the inconstancy of popular enthusiasm and resolution suggest that the best of statesmen might be frustrated because of their supporters' unreliability. Not even the great Pericles had been able to rely on their unswerving support, despite the strength of his personality and despite his consummate skill in exercising a restraint upon them compatible with freedom. 'The people giveth, and the people taketh away'. A great man may be worthy and able to rule, and the state may be best off in his hands, but his task is a particularly hard one if he has to frame his policies, and carry them into effect, through the medium of popular government. Cicero would deny to a politician so awkwardly placed the very possibility of the title of greatness. 'The man who depends on the mistaken plaudits of an ignorant populace is not to be numbered among the great', he says in his treatise on Moral Obligation.[7] Yet in a democracy, a man who respects the constitution has no option but to operate along constitutional lines. The path of the true tyrant is to that extent easier, if he is able to sweep aside the difficulties by the simple and convenient expedient of abolishing the constitution which gives rise to them.

All the same, there is a great deal of truth in what Machiavelli says in the fifth chapter of *Il Principe,* that it is through its own citizens that control of a state may be most easily secured. For one thing, there is a substantial degree of similarity in essence between a triumphant, militant democracy, and a triumphant, militant individual. Aristotle regarded this as a characteristic of extreme democracy, that is, when popular decrees and not the law constitute the supreme and final authority, that such a state 'is converted into a monarchy, that is, into the rule of an individual monarch composed of many individuals'.[8] 'A democracy of this description', Aristotle goes on, 'is analogous to tyranny among monarchical forms of government—in both the same character of rule, in both an exercise of despotic control over the better classes'. And indeed we ourselves speak in certain circumstances of the 'dictatorship of the proletariat', in which some people think to find the supreme good. Such a dictatorship or tyranny of the people practises the same ruthlessness with opposition as an individual tyrant, even though it is generally accounted for either as a proper expression of proletarian solidarity or as a defence of freedom against freedom's enemies, whether they be labelled fascists, revisionists, imperialists, or merely aristocrats. 'Ah Liberty, Liberty, what crimes are committed in thy name', cried Madame Roland. The quotation is familiar; but how many of us have really stopped to reflect upon its implications? The most exacting tyrannies are exercised allegedly in the defence of freedom, and the most thorough of inquisitions seeks only to safeguard the truth.

Yet in such a situation, as was apparent to Plato[9] and Aristotle, the borderline between the tyranny of the people and the tyranny of a dictator is a narrow one. The former makes possible the rise of a popular leader, who climbs to power on the enthusiasm of the multitude and, once supreme, converts his position into a personal despotism which may oppress as subjects those who were once his allies and supporters. To the Greek fourth century Dionysius I of Syracuse was the outstanding example. He was, as Aristotle points out, both demagogue and military leader, and this combination put a man in a very strong position. 'The great majority of ancient tyrants', Aristotle says,[10] 'had been demagogues', though in his own age of greater professionalism he felt the combination less likely than it once had been. He was to some extent guilty of anachronism, for in the archaic period a swing from democracy to tyranny was hardly possible, democracy not having been invented.[11] Archaic tyrannies seem to have evolved, in different places in different ways, as a factor in an attempt to broaden the basis of power in the state; the archaic antithesis was between tyranny and oligarchy. In the classical period the conflict between αὐτοκρατία (autocratic power) and ἰσοκρατία (equally shared power) was replaced by that which we have already examined, the conflict between ἀριστοκρατία (or ὀλιγαρχία), aristocracy, and δημοκρατία, democracy. Tyranny came to be not the product of a reaction to an exclusive oligarchy but the product of the astute management of an extreme democracy; the path to it lay *via* a trusting, frightened, or hoodwinked *demos,* and the philosophers, who were beginning to find the supreme virtues of government in a benevolent, wise, and enlightened despotism, were in no doubt of the extreme vices of its antipole. The Syracusans, in the crisis of 406–405, provided the example of the hoodwinked, frightened *demos*. The supremacy which Dionysius seized on the supposition that he alone was capable of defending Syracuse and eastern Sicily against Carthage he ultimately had to maintain by terror and by a 'divide-and-rule' manipulation of factional interests in his court and in the city at large. Far better, as Machiavelli expressly notes, if the leader, *il principe*—the prince, can rely on popular enthusiasm and affection, despite all the difficulties in which such reliance involves him, as I mentioned a little while ago. The surest tyranny, that is to say—and I use the word in its pure Greek sense—is to be founded on the 'personality cult' of the successful leader, born of positive respect and admiration, not of the panic of crisis, the disciplined obedience of indoctrination or the prompting of fear. Basically, that is to say, a parade of hundreds of thousands of chanting Red Guards waving copies of the *bons mots* of Mao Tse-tung is evidence of a *tyrannis* less sure in its essence than that afforded by unorganised and frantically excited teen-agers crying 'Lyndon we love you'. But, equally basically, both are manifestations of *tyrannides*. For although the *corruptio optimi* may be *pessima,* we must not forget what the *optimum* is. It is, and was, the enlightened tyranny which conceals itself, the ideal of the Augustan principate, the totality of the virtues of the Periclean régime, in name democracy, in practice the government of the leading man, and all the rest of it.

Such an arrangement requires two sides to make it—a leader who is *capax imperii* and willing to accept *imperium,* and a free people ready to surrender their freedom. And it is worth noting, as we proceed, that free peoples, much as they love their freedom, are to a remarkable degree of their own volition *proni in servitutem.* How often has a nation cast out one devil and swept and garnished its house only to find that seven devils worse than the first have come and taken up residence? For Aristotle's observation that democracy generally forms the starting-point for tyranny has held good through the millennia; popular revolutions and an excess of freedom have on significant occasions produced, within a few years, the new despotism of a single monarch. The French, Russian, and Chinese revolutions are notable cases in point, but many smaller instances are provided by countries such as Cuba, Haiti, the Latin-American republics, and, as seems to be the tendency, those of 'emerging Africa' also. This has nothing to do with development or under-development. The real point is that by nature, although people like and want personal liberty, they also like and want heroes and hero-worship. What in their various ways the Amphipolitans did for Brasidas, the Samians for Lysander, the Syracusans for Dion and Timoleon, others have done in *their* various ways ever since; their hopes and gratitudes have made favourites of their champions, and they have heaped on them heroic honours and prerogatives which in the end have allowed them to transcend and negate all that they once stood for.

This is not to say, of course, that a man may not be worthy of the popular enthusiasm and thoroughly deserve all that he gets out of it. But just as I mentioned that the arrangement requires two sides to make it, so it also requires the virtues of moderation in both sides—otherwise it will not work. A too volatile populace, or a cynical and selfish leader, will equally be ruinous of the *optimum* we have been discussing. If moderation is preserved—a sensible, balanced *demos* and a patriotic, unselfish leader—all is well. After all, a democracy must have its leaders, and they cannot lead unless the *demos* is to some extent prepared to place itself and its fortunes in their care. There have indeed been times when popular enthusiasm has been too eager to place full power in its leaders' hands. The people's hero-worship has in these cases become excessive and has had to be curbed by the good sense of the hero himself. The Roman populace tried to force on the Emperor Augustus the powers of the dictatorship, or a comprehensive 'oversight of the laws and of public and private conduct'. But such powers would have negated his concept of the Principate as in essence a traditional republican constitution reinforced with a few special safeguards. He declined the proffered powers, and was content with more modest prerogatives, much to the popular disappointment.[12] Similarly in 1672, when the coalition of Louis XIV and his allies had brought the Dutch Republic into so desperate a situation, the people clamoured for the overthrow of the government of Jan de Witt and the appointment to full command of William III, Prince of Orange. Their extremism in murdering Jan and Cornelis de Witt was not repudiated by the Prince, but he received with less equanimity the information of their insistence that he be accorded something more than the dignities of his forebears. Triumphant though he was, in the utter collapse of the mercantile oligarchy, he nevertheless answered more vehement demands to the effect that he 'preferred the position of Stadhouder, to which the state had raised him, to that of Sovereign, and . . . felt himself bound in honour and conscience not to put interest before duty'.[13]

The necessary limits are not easy for either side to draw. William and Augustus were shrewd enough to know where, for the common good and for their own, it was proper to draw them. In the case of Athens, Thucydides judged that Pericles did not overstep them; but there were others who judged differently. Thucydides also seems of the opinion (though this remains uncertain) that Alcibiades *did* transgress the desirable bounds; but equally it may be possible to argue that he did not. Where the limits are correctly drawn and maintained, the product is a mild, beneficent personal *tyrannis* within a democratic framework, and although the character of the phenomenon may to some extent have changed, we may see the signs of it in our own society on both sides of the Atlantic. Trends, parties, programmes, are regularly transformed into an identification with *people*. This is not new; it has always been so. Mass media of communication have no more than enhanced it. Government has become personal in a manner which, in a democratic society, I believe to be frequently undesirable and potentially dangerous. The Labour administrations in Britain in 1964 and 1966 were to a considerable degree carried into and sustained in office by the personal capacities, as favourably appraised by the electorate, of the leader of the Labour party; and the party's stock began to lapse as the personal appeal of the Prime Minister, as he had then become, began for various reasons to lose its lustre in the eyes of many who had supported his government. It would be unjust to judge the merits or shortcomings of the British government at that period solely with reference to the merits or shortcomings of Harold Wilson, but his personality must play a substantial part in any such judgement because of the effect upon the voters that it had undoubtedly produced. To many people he personally represented, or came to represent, Socialist Britain, and what were regarded, according to one's point of view, as the virtues or vices of practical Socialism tended to be laid at his personal door. Similarly, a particular right-wing brand of conservatism in the United States rapidly became 'Goldwaterism' because Senator Goldwater happened to be its best (though by no means its most extreme) exponent. President Johnson did not, in his years of office, give rise to any new '-ism', but he was generally regarded, and customarily referred to, as personifying the spirit of his own administration.

Allied with this tendency to 'personalise' issues is an inclination to popular *dynastic* thinking. This affection for a dynasty, coupled with the tendency towards personification, lurks as a basic and natural phenomenon even in the most egalitarian society. It became especially visible, for example, as an element in the appeal of what may be called the Kennedy group. For although this group, or *factio,* as the Romans would have called it, relied very properly, and according to the traditional pattern of American politics, on a sound basis of *clientela* judiciously located, it capitalised on a wider sentiment to the extent that John Kennedy's death produced a particular popular reaction widely commented on by observers. This was a deeply felt, perhaps vague and unformulated but very powerful conviction that his mantle might be expected to descend to one of his younger brothers, maybe ultimately to both, Lyndon Johnson being a kind of interloper into whose hands, by constitutional accident, the inheritance had been diverted.[14]

To sum up, therefore: the parallel ideas of liberty and hero-worship, particularly well exemplified in a special union, during the 1960's, in the hero-cult of John F. Kennedy, fulfil evident human needs and can, indeed should, coexist. The individual in pursuit of power may ignore or may profit from these ideas. If he ignores them, seizing his power by a coup d'état or through a military crisis, and maintaining himself as a military despot, he can scarcely avoid becoming the worst kind of tyrant, and his tyranny is unlikely to survive longer than his personal ability to impose it. Another sort of would-be tyrant may indeed reach his position because a grateful people has put him there, but through selfishness or vanity he may abuse the trust and end by depriving the people of their liberty and himself of their adulation. But it is with the third sort of powerful individual that we must be concerned. We have seen what are to be the bases of his power—his own capacities and the popular enthusiasm. The word 'tyrant' may be used of him by his opponents or in jest, but his leadership— which we can hardly call 'rule'—will have nothing in it that is tyrannical in any accepted sense. His command will rely on the hearts and affections of men, and on their service to him freely given and generously responded to. There have been many men, of very different characters, who may be said to fall into this group, and we may all think of examples for ourselves. Such a man, for instance,

was Winston Churchill, or Giuseppe Garibaldi, or George
Washington. Such a man, if we go back to the Greek world
with which we are concerned, was Timoleon, or Pericles,
or—I am now prepared to suggest—Alcibiades.

In terms of chronology, Book VIII of Thucydides gives us
very little of Alcibiades' career. Books V-VII provide a
greater span, from his first entry on the scene in the affair
of the Spartan ambassadors in 420 to his flight to Sparta.
Xenophon covers his final years in the *Hellenica,* and
Plutarch has left us his biography. But the eighth book
of Thucydides contains much of the greatest significance in
any attempt to assess the character of this remarkable man,
and gives us a unique picture of his search after a successful
return to the power he wanted and had once enjoyed in
his native city. 'Everything has been said about Alcibiades',
it was once remarked to me; and yet there is all to say. As
we have seen, he excited controversy in his lifetime. It is
clear from Plato, from Lysias, from Isocrates, and from the
fourth speech attributed to Andocides, that he continued to
excite controversy after his death. The verdict, with all
acknowledgment of Alcibiades' personal accomplishments
and undoubted qualities, or sometimes with denial of them,
generally turns out to be hostile. It is not often that one sees
anything as frankly laudatory as McGregor's treatment.
But whether laudatory or not, the verdict is the product of
Alcibiades' effect on others. It is, as we have seen, a natural
consequence of the possession of the ingredients of power—
kratos, dynamis, gnome, periousia, time, and so forth—that
phthonos and *echthos* are aroused in others. Alcibiades, who
did indeed possess these attributes and ingredients to a
remarkable degree, also evoked the natural response to a

remarkable degree. What we see, therefore, we tend to see through the distorted vision of our informants, some of whom were at enmity with him, and others of whom found it hard to reconcile a personal liking of the man with a dislike of what he was and what he did. We see the *enfant terrible,* the clever *dilettante,* the amateur who could outdo the professionals, the gambler who ruined his country as well as himself, the man who, as Quintilian said of Ovid, preferred to indulge his genius rather than control it.[15] It is unusual, as was said at the outset, to try and look at things from his point of view, but I believe McGregor to be right when he says that 'at all stages of his career Alcibiades knew exactly what he was doing and did it with deliberation'.[16] There is much in him that reminds one of Themistocles—a κράτιστος γνώμων and ἄριστος εἰκαστής,[17] and it has been well said that ability to predict the future responses of men and likely course of events is the hallmark of the great leader. It is thus evident that our approach to the problem of Alcibiades and power must be from Alcibiades' side.

It is significant that Aristophanes makes Dionysus say, in the *Frogs,* [18] that the city longs for Alcibiades, hates him, and wants to have him. No clearer expression of what we now call a love-hate relationship could be devised. It was a mutual relationship. Alcibiades knew what he was worth;[19] although in his heart of hearts he believed democracy nonsense (and I take his famous remark at Sparta to reflect his personal conviction), he wanted his power to come, as it had come to Pericles, through popular esteem and by popular will. This is an element in the complicated manoeuvres of his return in 411–410 which is of major importance and should not be lost sight of. The Athenians could never quite trust him, and he could never quite trust them. He knew from experience the truth about the *demos* that Edmund Burke was later to enunciate,[20] that 'having looked to government for bread, on the very first scarcity they will turn and bite the hand that fed them'; he was to experience it again. But he could have confidence in no one else, and neither could they. This was the tragic dilemma. We cannot say that it ruined Athens, for there were other factors in Athens' fall than this; but we can say that it was the cause of failure to save her.

Plutarch pairs his Greek biography of Alcibiades with his Roman biography of Coriolanus. The parallelism is more revealing than Plutarch brings out. The superficial link of circumstance between the two is of course that both men were exiled from their cities after playing leading roles in them, that both joined their cities' enemies and gave those enemies powerful reinforcement, and that in the end both came to repentance. But Plutarch's lives generally exemplify, for the edification of posterity, particular human characteristics in their subjects. The common characteristic between Alcibiades and Coriolanus—would one call it virtue or vice?—is that of 'pride'. Plutarch leaves vague the terms in which he might have framed this, for the *Comparatio* which rounds off the pair of lives is uninformative on this score. The choice of word would however be significant; our 'pride' does not adequately convey the nuances of the possible Greek (or Latin) alternatives, and our interpretation will affect, and will be affected by, what we choose. There are two Latin possibilities. *Arrogantia,* or *superbia?* In Greek we have a choice of three. Ὑπερηφανία perhaps? Or φιλοτιμία? Or μεγαλοψυχία? No man can fulfil any characteristic entirely and to the exclusion of others, but it is remarkable to what an extent, if we take the last two of the terms I quoted, we can evolve a composite picture of Alcibiades from what Aristotle says in the *Nicomachean Ethics* about the φιλότιμος and the μεγαλόψυχος.[21] It is worth reminding ourselves of what was said in the first chapter about Thomas Hobbes and his 'gallant man', the 'man of pride'.[22] The μεγαλόψυχος, the man with the great *psyche,* is not 'proud' in any sense of ours, but the term is conventional and I will use it as such. 'High-minded' has been tried, but is equally unsatisfactory. The proud man knows his own worth; this is fundamental, and was so in Alcibiades' case. Knowing his own merits, which are not imaginary but undoubted, he has great self-esteem and seeks the reward of his merits as his due. What is this reward? To obtain honour on condition of deserving it. That is to say, he is able, he knows he is able, he wishes others to confide in his ability, he wishes to requite that confidence with success, and he wishes to receive the honour success has deserved. He is an admirable candidate for that third type of tyranny I outlined earlier. He can operate to good effect in democracy, for (again to quote Burke) success is the only infallible criterion of wisdom to vulgar judgements.[23] When he receives honour, Aristotle points out, his pleasure will not be unmixed, because he knows he is only receiving his due —but it is the best they have to give, and as such he accepts it. He despises paltry adulation, and equally he despises paltry contempt. He is frank in his hatreds and friendships, cares for truth more than the opinions of men, is consistently truthful save that for popular consumption he may say less than he thinks. These are some of the characteristics of the 'proud man'; but in Alcibiades' case they did not stand alone, and the admixture of some element of Aristotle's *philotimos,* the 'ambitious' man whose pursuit of *time* may be excessive, gave his personality an additional complication.

The child is father to the man, and it is fashionable to look for the basis of personality, and therefore of public and private behaviour, in a man's upbringing and youthful environment. It is, I suppose, generally agreed that his education in Pericles' household affected Alcibiades deeply; Plutarch stresses this, and rightly so.[24] In that company, surrounded by the new learning, the most interesting people, the whole atmosphere of artistic and political excellence, Alcibiades derived a certain freedom from inhibition, to which McGregor draws attention.[25] He also came to know his own worth, as the essential basis for his career (as we have already noted), and to know what he must aim for and how, by capitalising on his talents, he must aim for it. These, then, are two principal ingredients of power in the individual—self-appreciation and determination. Alcibiades had both, and—also essential—he had the talents with which he could organise his programme and advance to his goal. The basic pattern, as H. D. Lasswell has pointed out,[26] is that a man pursues what he values through the institutions he lives with on the basis of the resources he commands. 'That men want power is a statement', he says, 'we can accept as true in every society where power exists; this is not to say whether everybody wants it with the same intensity'. But for those who want it there are certain bases, and Alcibiades, in addition to self-esteem, determination, and innate talent, had a large number of the possible bases that Lasswell proceeds to list—physical ability, wealth, enlightenment, skill, social position, affection. They gave him the requisite *dynamis* and that in turn produced the necessary *kratos*. Indeed, we may find in Alcibiades as an individual all those basic elements of power which we diagnosed in a powerful city, when we were investigating the power of the Athenian democracy. Plato was right, we may well conclude, when he framed his *Republic* around the supposition that the way to investigate δικαιοσύνη (justice) in the individual human being was to investigate it in a *polis*.

From this we may go on to argue that, in pursuit of power and in defence of it, Alcibiades might act in all the ways laid down in our study of Thucydides' own analysis of power. 'Honour, security and self-interest' will prompt his actions, and we must regard action taken for these causes as natural.[27] It was natural, that is to say, for a man of his talents, his *dynamis* and his *megalopsychia*, to aim for power, to possess it insofar as he could, and to exercise it when he had got it. If in exercising it he happened to exercise it for the benefit of someone else besides himself—his city, for example—he deserved some extra credit. This consideration may be the clue to that difficult remark of Thucydides in VIII 86, 4, when the Athenians in Samos were wanting to sail to the Piraeus and dispose of the oligarchs, to the effect that 'Alcibiades seems then for the first time to have rendered a service to his country inferior to that of no man'. Sir Frank Adcock saw in the statement Thucydides' indication that Alcibiades was turning over a new leaf, and thought that it implied criticism of his former conduct towards his city.[28] But power and its use, we must remember, are not only natural to the city or individual capable of them; they are without moral content. It is only method that is open to criticism, and Thucydides is not criticising method here. He is no more than stating a fact as he sees it, without any imputation that Alcibiades had been wrong hitherto and that he was going to be more right in the future. What he does imply, if he implies anything, is the additional credit a powerful city (or individual) earns if he exercises his power with gratuitous unselfishness.

I have suggested that Alcibiades, from his youth up, approved of the type of *tyrannis* enjoyed by Pericles, that he wished to contrive such a *tyrannis* for himself, that he had the capacity for it, that he knew he had, and that he almost fulfilled the character of the proud man which Aristotle defined as the chief adornment of the virtues.[29] I also advocated that his attitude to affairs must be judged in the same light, with reference to the acquisition of his *tyrannis,* as that of the Athenian democracy itself. But there were obstacles in his way, and these proved in the end to have a counter-power of their own too great for Alcibiades' efforts and planning. Some of these obstacles were external to him, and others were inherent in him. One of the former, quite simply, was his lack of uniform success. To remain an effective leader a man must be prepared to pull a succession of rabbits, real or apparent, out of the hat. Alcibiades began well in 420 and continued with reasonable success for the next five years. The defeat of Syracuse and conquest of Sicily, which he so ardently advocated, would have been the biggest, most triumphant, rabbit of all. In a private capacity such ostentatious triumphs as his performance at the Olympic Games of 416 had the same end in view.[30] He knew well enough what he had to do. Yet at crucial moments he was deprived of the power to implement what he had begun and to reap the fruit of his planning. He planned the final confrontation with Sparta, but the last, all-important battle at Mantinea was left to the leadership of others and was lost. His recall from Syracuse may have been ruinous to the expedition; Thucydides seems to have thought so, and if, as P. A. Brunt believes, the thought was prompted by Alcibiades, then Alcibiades thought so too.[31] What he began in 410—the reconstitution of the Athenian empire— was equally taken out of his hands and spoiled through none of his fault. His famous celebration of the Eleusinian mysteries of 407 showed that the Olympic victor of 416 had not lost his touch, but he was not allowed to follow through what he had begun with such *éclat*.

'Between craft and credulity', said Burke, 'the voice of reason is stifled.'[23] Alcibiades' γνώμη *should* have suc-ceeded, and the people ought to have believed; but, as we have seen, they did not. The second obstacle in Alcibiades' way was the constant hostility, the φθόνος and ἔχθος, which the state or the man of power naturally meets. He could never quite overcome it; he reacted to it with a natural anger and frustration. When he heard that the city had condemned him to death in his absence, he remarked 'I will show them that I'm alive all right'.[33] But he knew the phenomena, and his manoeuvres in Book VIII to bring about his recall well illustrate that he diagnosed them and capitalised on them. Judging the Athenians' needs for his talents and their basic awareness of them, and judging also that aid from Persia had become a useful lever for the pur-pose, he was able to see that the hostility of the *demos* to the oligarchs was, or would become, greater than their hostility to himself. His complex arrangements first to help the oligarchy into power and then to help in sabotaging it, which Thucydides records in their entirety, are, as McGregor rightly saw, one of the best pieces of evidence for Alcibiades' outstanding gifts.[34] Yet even after that his position was only temporarily secure. After 407 he did not bother to try. 'There is,' to quote Edmund Burke yet once more,[35] 'a limit at which forbearance ceases to be a virtue'. Even so, he was still prepared in 405 to warn the Athenian commanders in the Hellespont against the folly of their situation; his warning was rejected with scorn, but Alcibiades still proved himself the κράτιστος γνώμων: the consequence of the rejection was the final disaster of Aegospotami.

One of the personal obstacles to the successful pursuit of power in Alcibiades' case was a characteristic which I think I can only describe as imprudence. Of course, as long as he did the right things in public he could be as cynical as he wanted in private. There can be as little doubt that he was guilty of profanation of the Mysteries as that he was innocent of the mutilation of the Hermae.[36] The difficulty is that a public man finds it hard to be private. In a comparatively small and intimate society like the Greek *polis,* and in the case of so bizarre and striking a figure as Alcibiades, this is understandable. It is equally true nowadays, although for different reasons. The newspapers, radio, and television often carry to unpleasant and at times reprehensible extremes their invasion of privacy on the basis of a contention that 'the public has a right to know'. That absolute right, as so stated, may be—indeed is—open to dispute; but a politician must expect that he, his family, and his activities will to a great degree become public property. In embarking upon a political career this is a hazard he has to accept as part of the bargain, and he does so, presumably, with his eyes open. He and his friends must be prepared to guard their conduct accordingly. Alcibiades ought, therefore, to have exercised a greater restraint than he did. Had he done so, he would have created fewer misgivings and so lessened the hostility which we have already considered. Even today, cynical levity towards organised religion would not endear a man to the generality of the electorate. Other follies and pranks could be accepted and were almost enjoyed by the Athenians, as they would be now; but to overstep the mark can be fatal, and it *was* fatal for Alcibiades.

We might include in this list of flaws in Alcibiades' armoury the lack of patriotism and the general moral turpitude of which he has been accused. By the latter we should, I think, mean no more than that he attracted women and was prepared to take advantage of the fact. Despite a lingering streak of puritanism in modern thinking,[37] we are more tolerant in such matters than our forebears and may well conclude that such a charge against Alcibiades is inadmissible. In the great ones of history we positively admire and enjoy a leavening of healthy heterosexual promiscuity—we welcome it, in fact. Caesar and Napoleon made conquests other than on the battlefield, and we warm to them the more as human beings. Alcibiades, like Mussolini, had his mistress with him at the time of his assassination, and it adds a *tendresse* to the final tragedy. His seduction of the wife of King Agis of Sparta increases our appreciation of and respect for his superb panache.[38] Alexander the Great, on the contrary, in whom Tarn claimed it as a virtue that he was not interested in women,[39] seems by comparison cold and rather repellent. Now this does not mean that a political or military hero ought in his spare time to be a philanderer, or that a great leader must also be a great lover. But if a man cannot win the confidence and affection of one half of the population (whose approach to him, as the psychologists warn us, must from the nature of things contain an element of the sexual instinct, whether conscious or not), then he cannot fulfil all the necessary criteria for the good *tyrannos*.

Alcibiades' lack of patriotism is an issue which may be reserved for later consideration.[40] It is perhaps unjust to describe his escape to Sparta in such terms; certainly this was his own view. The efforts of his enemies and the vehemence of his own nature seem to have left him no alternative.[41] If his action is held to show apparent inconsistency with his previous conduct, we should remember that a re-thinking of his way of life was forced on him, and in these circumstances Cicero held that to be inconsistent was no vice.[42] But this is an age in which it is openly maintained that a man's moral conduct is a matter for his own conscience and no concern of his neighbours, and when patriotism is liable to be regarded as one of those rather old-fashioned virtues of a moribund establishment. What is more, we have just concluded that the pursuit or defence of power lacks moral connotation, and that in responding to the laws of power Alcibiades cannot therefore be properly criticised by the use of moral criteria. If this is so, neither the climate of current thinking nor the tenor of our present arguments makes this a propitious context in which to undertake a consideration of that particular issue.

Chapter 5

On this occasion, however, as on so many others, the Lacedaemonians proved themselves to be the most convenient enemies that the Athenians could possibly have had. For the two peoples were of very different characters, the one quick and the other slow, the one enterprising, the other deficient in a readiness to take risks. And this was of very considerable advantage to the Athenians—the more so because their empire was a maritime one.

Thucydides VIII 96, 5

It is the function of an aristocracy which disposes of large resources and enjoys a large measure of liberty to prevent abuses and disorder by means of a strict self-discipline.

B. de Jouvenel, *Le Pouvoir*, 296

No republic can remain forever quiet and enjoy its freedom within its narrow frontiers.

G. Ritter, *The Corrupting Influence of Power*, 38

War is not merely a political act but also a real political instrument, a continuation of political commerce, a carrying out of the same by other means.

C. von Clausewitz, *On War*, Bk. I, Chap. 1

Power and the Military Machine

IN earlier chapters I have tried to demonstrate that power essentially consists in an ascendancy over others, derived from an accumulation of certain qualities flourishing in a favourable environment. Thucydides illustrates the phenomenon at the outset of his work. 'Vixere fortes ante Agamemnona multi,' said Horace,[1] 'sed omnes illacrimabiles urgentur ignotique longa nocte': with Agamemnon everything came right, and Homer and History remembered him as the commander of the greatest expression of Hellenic power ever seen in an earlier age.[2] I remarked earlier that power could only be realised when it expressed itself in its actual exercise, and that that actual exercise had, in Agamemnon's case, taken the form of a great military enterprise against Troy. Power, that is to say, may be and frequently is expressed in its clearest sense in war. One stronger power may follow the law of gods and men, to which Athens appealed, and enforce its will on a weaker power; or two powers of equal strength, both following that other natural law (which we have examined on a previous occasion) that power must expand, come into collision—a collision which will decide which one goes on to greater strength and which must give way and fall into decline.[3] Such a collision was the conflict which Thucydides was recording, and from the very start he judged the impact of it to be such that even the Persian wars would appear to be of less consequence.[4]

Nevertheless, warfare is not the inevitable product of power, nor a necessary demonstration of it. Power consists, after all, in having the ability to ensure that others are prepared to do what you want them to do. It is, as we have seen, a matter of being δυνατός and κράτιστος. The *kratos* and *dynamis* need not consist in the physical strength of an individual person or the military might of a city or nation. They can be represented by admirable qualities of character, by *res gestae* which evoke gratitude and recognition, by moral and intellectual distinction, all of which may give a man or a group or an entire people an ascendancy gladly conceded by the rest of their fellows. But the effective existence of power, however derived, can only be seen when others are actually doing what the possessor of the power wishes them to do; successful power produces evident results. There can, in the end, be no such thing as unsuccessful power, as many a despot has learned to his cost—for where results are not produced potential power remains unrealised, and where success is replaced by later lack of success actual power is negated. In both cases the result is the same, for when power cannot expand it must contract.[5]

It has emerged from what has been said earlier that the existence of authority, of rulers and ruled, is a kind of divine law integral to human life. Power is natural and its exercise inescapable, whether we like it or not. The dogma of the Melian Dialogue, which formed one of the bases from which this discussion set out, has not been invalidated by anything we have yet seen. The best that society has been able to do is to mitigate the crudity of such a doctrine, to acknowledge as desirable the ultimate force of high ideals, and to exhibit a preference for benevolent power as being most acceptable to mankind and, in consequence, the most permanent and useful type of power. The wise statesman, the tolerant majority, the acquiescent minority, the city or nation content to be *primus inter pares* in a commonwealth of friendly states, all paying due attention to ideals of justice and unselfishness—in this way the laws of power are canalised into something tolerable for the peaceful organisation of society. Those who defer to the authority in question do so because they have agreed or contracted to do so, or because they want to; and they reap the benefit of having some recognition of what they sometimes call their 'rights' accorded to them. But what happens when power is not benevolent, when dynasties outlive their welcome or cities or nations fail to enlist their subjects in willing cooperation? And what happens when a government or commonwealth, however peaceable itself, is faced with a challenge to its physical existence or to the existence of the ideals its people cherish? In the former case, when power ceases to be benevolent, one might say that the best principles are lacking; but other principles of power are there to which there remains an appeal. In the latter case, when there is a challenge of force, it becomes evident that benevolence and pacific, moral ascendancy are insufficient. In all the cases power, faced with a challenge to its supremacy and continuance, must assert itself in a direct form.

This may be most easily seen, in a British context, in the regular experience of the private citizen. He pays, it is fair to say, a great deal more income tax than he wishes to pay or approves of paying. But having been born into his community, and having by remaining in it accepted voluntarily

to continue a member of it, he also accepts that the power of
the community, vested in certain representatives of the
whole population, to demand money of him is valid in its
operation. He therefore pays up. He is exhorted to do so,
from time to time, by Her Majesty's Inspector of Taxes; if
he does not, the Inspector will follow up his exhortation
with a note beginning with the ominous phrase 'Dear Sir,
Unless . . .': that is, a polite request to pay is replaced by a
threat of consequences should payment be withheld. In a
real and physical sense, therefore, a British citizen may be
seized by other representatives of the community, that is, a
policeman or two, and deprived of his personal liberty.
'*Force majeure*' will have been applied to him. Translate
this into terms of the members of the Delian League, the
φόρος (tribute), the τάκται or assessors of tribute, the
ἐγλογεῖς φόρου or collectors of tribute,[6] and the revolts
which, Thucydides tells us, resulted in δουλεία, or depri-
vation of liberty,[7] and you have the very same situation in
the community of the Athenian Empire. When the allies
refused to pay the *phoros* which they had contracted to pay,
Athens was able, in virtue of her power, to apply *force
majeure,* and in the end they were compelled to subscribe.
The Athenians were not anxious to do this; one must not
suppose that holders of power who exercise it in terms of
violence do so because they like it, or do so as a first resort.
The parent who tells his small son, just before he applies the
slipper to the youthful backside, that 'this is going to hurt
me more than it will hurt you' is not necessarily being
hypocritical. But it does mean that in the last resort power
must be successfully applicable in this form, strong enough

physically to defend itself against rivals or to administer chastisement to inferiors.

If a powerful city finds itself obliged to use force against a recalcitrant subject or challenging rival one might argue that it must have shown a deficiency in one of the five essentials, in *gnome,* which had allowed the situation to get so far out of hand. But such events may be beyond its ability, even with the best-laid plans, to prevent. Benevolence, as Cleon warned, may be taken for weakness, and an element of toughness may be required to maintain respect. In any case it may be suggested that such an argument hardly matters. *Kratos* is *kratos,* and *dynamis* is *dynamis.* Whether people obey because they want to, or because they are afraid not to, or because they are forcibly compelled, the end result, obedience, is the same and the power is the same of which obedience is the fruit. It is also regrettably unlikely that the ascendancy gained by benevolence, enthusiasm, and all the fine elements that make up the best kind of exercise of power, can be indefinitely maintained. Popularity is transient, and gratitude is the most short-lived of human emotions. The result is that *force majeure,* the ability to compel successfully, is a necessary adjunct of power. 'If you don't do as I say, I will knock you down' is a crude and, in a civilised society, deplorable attitude: but if we are honest with ourselves we must admit that it is society's final sanction when the forces of persuasion, moral pressure, religious restraint, and so forth have proved unavailing. When power has to defend itself against assault this is necessarily invoked as the only existing sanction, and is justified, in the general estimate, on moral and religious grounds. But keeping to our denial of a moral element in power we may leave such grounds of justification aside and claim that violence in the interest of power is, on Thucydides' evaluation, only reprehensible when the violence is gratuitous. Of course, by *force majeure* or violence, βία, I am not necessarily meaning actual physical force actually used. The threat may be enough, or it may express itself along humanitarian channels—that is, you do not necessarily flog prisoners to cure them of their naughty ways but you send them to rehabilitation centres or put them on probation. But the prisoner so dealt with is nevertheless forcibly controlled (ἀρχόμενος βίᾳ): in the final analysis the basis is what I have described.

The failure of the Athenians to maintain their power in the late fifth century was in the end, as we saw, due to a breakdown of the five essential elements which compose it—*kratos, dynamis, gnome, periousia,* and *tharsos.* In physical terms this failure was expressed by a failure to win the final battle. The last battle, and indeed all the battles, were no more than a projection into terms of physical conflict of the power conflict out of which the war had arisen. Von Clausewitz, whose most famous dictum (in its correct form, for it is often misquoted) precedes this chapter, also observed that 'War is a conflict of great interests which is settled by bloodshed, and only in that is it different from others'.[8] War is, therefore, only one aspect of the wider, natural antagonism between rival powers or between rulers and ruled. It is, however, evident in general that the power well capable of waging war successfully is in a strong position as regards maintaining itself. If we put this into the terms of the Peloponnesian War, it means that the city which *could* win battles, and was well trained and equipped to do so, had a marked advantage. In its military strength it had a firm source of *kratos* and *dynamis*. This gave it, at least in the department of physical superiority on the battlefield, a definite *periousia:* and because of this the city might well possess comfortable reserves of *tharsos*. Only *gnome* remains unprovided for. But battles are not won without the *gnome* of the commander, and if a military power is successful one must suppose its presence. Von Clausewitz listed[9] three elements as composing what he called 'the chief moral power in war': these were '(i) the talents of the commander, (ii) the military virtue of the army, and (iii) the army's national feeling'. It is in the light of these considerations, and of all that, in this long general analysis, we have postulated about power expressed in military terms, that we must go on to consider *the* city which in Hellas best exemplified them—Sparta.

Sparta's international reputation and influence had been founded on her military prowess, and that prowess in its turn had been founded on the military preparedness required by the curious and uncomfortable structure of the Spartan state. The community of Spartiatai, in the classical period, apparently amounted to not more than one sixteenth or so of the total population of Laconia and Messenia.[10] Because of this *oliganthropia* the Spartans' achievements seemed all the more remarkable. It formed the very understandable and justifiable starting-point for Xenophon in his treatise on the *Politeia of the Lacedaemonians:* 'Reflecting on an occasion that Sparta, though one of the cities which possesses very restricted manpower, is nevertheless most powerful and renowned in Hellas, I fell to wondering how this came about'.[11] He soon found the answer. 'When, however, I thought about the way in which the Spartiatai are trained, my amazement evaporated. Or rather, it concentrated on Lycurgus, who was their lawgiver, for it is through his laws that they have attained their felicity.' The Spartan system of education, which prolonged itself into a lifetime habit of training and self-discipline, was designed to overcome, and to a great extent did overcome, the difficulties inherent in the Spartan situation. By that discipline, and by their readiness to meet any unrest, the Spartans maintained their precarious supremacy. By it their numbers possessed a greater value than that of a simple count of heads. By it they could keep in subjection the lower classes whose labour, by a kind of vicious circle, alone made it practicable.

In the end, however, it was (as Aristotle expressly observes)[12] *oliganthropia* which was one of the major factors contributive to the undoing of Spartan pre-eminence in the fourth century. The system ultimately failed—not because it was not applied, or was misapplied, but because of the inability of the small governing class to be self-perpetuating. The process was assisted by other defects for which there is classical evidence. A total self-abnegation was required of all Spartiatai. They had to renounce all interest in money, in luxury, in acquisition of wealth. They existed not for their own profit but for the common good of the state. The good of the state suffered if the Spartiate control of the Helots and perioikoi, or indeed of themselves, was in any way weakened. This total surrender to the state was an enormous thing to require. It needed the complete and thorough organisation of the individual by the state. It presupposed that the ultimate good lay only within the borders of Laconia and Messenia, and therefore any outside influence was liable to corrupt. A wind of change might blow across the borders, encouraging the Helots and perioikoi to unrest, and infecting the Spartiatai with sordid, self-seeking notions about looking after number one. Hence the well-known measures of expelling foreigners which were taken from time to time; hence a certain unwillingness to enter into commitments abroad which would enable too many Spartans to get a liking for the fleshpots of the iniquitous world outside. As Kitto remarks, 'a contemporary parallel may suggest itself to the unenlightened'.[13]

Yet it is a logical position. If you live in what is for you the best possible of all worlds, external influences *must* be corrupting, and it is essential to protect the people from them. It is also essential to inculcate them with the pure doctrine, so that they will not even *want* to hanker after the meretricious glitter of dirty capitalism, Western degeneracy, or whatever one may term it. What impressed Xenophon was not only Spartan discipline but Spartan acceptance of it. To this, insulation was undoubtedly the key.[14] History provides more than one example of the Spartan gone to the bad, from love of money or power or both, but Pausanias, the victor of Plataea, will suffice as an instance of the occurrence. Aristotle notes how one effect of the decline in numbers, allied apparently to the working of the inheritance system, had been that land-holdings became unequal, and the ownership of land had fallen into the hands of a few. Furthermore, he says, because of the number of heiresses and the practice of giving large dowries, two fifths of the land was in the possession of females. Both Aristotle and Plutarch observe[15] that Lycurgus' regulations had less effect on the women than on the men, and the worship of wealth, which Aristotle claims as prevalent in later fourth-century Sparta, was in no small part due, in his opinion, to the 'unrestrained and indiscriminate licence and luxury indulged in by the women'. Xenophon, whose final remarks about Sparta show his disappointment in the decline of pristine standards, ascribes the responsibility to the spirit of acquisition, τὸ κεκτῆσθαι.[16]

Nevertheless, one must allow that Lycurgus, or his system if we may allow his name to stand for what was the finished product of a lengthy evolution, tried hard. After all, no system until our own day has been as successful in dragooning a whole people from cradle to grave in such thorough-going personal subjection to the state's demands. It needed the decline in numbers as well as the decline in standards to overthrow it. The latter in itself might not have been ruinous, and instances of it might have been checked and kept in isolation. It seems to me that it is not the ultimate failure of the Spartan system that is surprising—it is the length of its success. This may indeed be the final verdict of posterity over modern equivalents in which private inclination and the liberty of the individual are suppressed in the common interest of the system. The key, as Xenophon rightly saw, lay in the ἐπιτηδεύματα.[17] It had to. It may have been possible for the chamaeleon-like Alcibiades to show himself *plus Spartiate que les Spartiates* and to throw himself into the spirit and practice of the Lycurgan régime; it increases one's admiration of him to read how he did so. But he was an exception. The only real way to get the Spartiatai to endure their system was to make sure that they never knew any other, and to start them off at the earliest possible age.

They would thus grow up with their habits and ideas formed in the common mould, thinking no more and no less than the state required, in the way the state required. Any later than the earliest possible age would be too late. The great danger is that of disillusion; the reaction to disillusion can be extreme, and this may help to explain why, when they got the opportunity, some carefully brought up Spartans did go so thoroughly to the bad. But even so, it may be that we stress these instances too much. When Xenophon admired the Spartan training, it was the general effect that he admired no less than the principle behind it.

The stifling of reaction involved, then, three virtues. Those of discipline and obedience are the cardinal Spartan virtues with which everyone is familiar.[18] There is, however, a third characteristic about the Spartan upbringing or *agoge,* the inculcation of which a Spartiate would have regarded as a necessary virtue, although it does not seem to have been much emphasised in discussion on these topics. It is the virtue of emulation or rivalry.[19] In the modern age it may seem an unwelcome and unworthy object of education. When the freedom of the individual is held to be a greater good than discipline, and when it is more fashionable to question authority than to obey it, it is not surprising that egalitarianism and a hostility towards distinction, even if deserved, is preferred to a rivalry that acts as an incentive to greater effort. But this sort of rivalry the Spartiates were taught to cultivate. Many of their athletic exercises were based on the rivalry of different groups of young men trying to outdo one another. Although the background of the society was that all Spartiates were *Homoioi,* 'equals', and although this was strictly maintained in practice as well as in theory, it was fostered by a determination always to do better than the next man. In the Spartan ephebate the selection of boys for each *agela* was just as rigorous and just as cruel in its way as the selection for fraternities used to be in some American universities; and the experiences which the beginner had to undergo were as vexatious and humiliating as anything which a fag at an English public school or a freshman at a German or Dutch university ever had to face even in the worst periods of these institutions.

As a result of these virtues, there was created for Sparta a *kratos,* and in consequence a *dynamis,* which necessarily influenced her neighbours. Spartan foreign policy in the sixth century had expressed itself in the creation of a system of alliances directed at the preservation of the Spartan state.[20] This system formed a kind of *cordon sanitaire* around Laconia and Messenia. It served Spartan *deos* and *ōphelia,* and inevitably gave the Spartans, throughout the Greek world and beyond, a great deal of *time.*[21] Sparta's allies subscribed more or less willingly to her *arche,* for they got protection out of it and were not, as it seems, oppressed. Together they constituted the most formidable and most permanent organisation the Hellas of city-states ever knew. Profiting from all this, Sparta was in the fifth century a 'satisfied power'. All that was necessary for her was to maintain the existing situation. But power, as already emphasised, is not static; if it does not expand it must contract. While Athenian *dynamis* became more and more dynamic, and in the process increased itself, that of Sparta was likely to decline. It was to face these circumstances and to halt such a decline that the Spartans, unable to accomplish this by any other means, had recourse to war in 431.[22]

The quality of Spartan power was limited in the sense that it expressed itself only in the ability to win battles, and that the end for which the battles were won lacked any expansionist characteristic. Thucydides is at pains to emphasise, as was mentioned in an earlier chapter,[23] that ὄψις, visual appearance, was no guide to the reality or character of that power. On such a criterion, he suggests, one would be in danger of overestimating the power of Athens and underestimating that of Sparta, judging from the evident beauty and grandeur of the one and from the lack of architectural significance or merit of the other. Looking at the same sites today one could make the same mistake, as Thucydides foretold. What was the real guide to its character was its ability to provide that protection for Sparta and her allies which had been its foundation and strength. In view of the rise of Athens, the Corinthians among others began to have doubts about this ability, and in their important speech at the first Congress of Sparta the Corinthian delegation very rightly emphasised the difference between the Athenian and Spartan temperaments.[24] Benevolent apathy will not perpetuate a power which must always renew itself if it is to remain effective. The essence of the situation is that Sparta, while still undoubtedly possessing *kratos* and *dynamis,* is showing herself deficient in *gnome* through persistent non-recognition of the danger Athens provides, and deficient in *tharsos* if, having had it brought to her notice, she does not take appropriate action. The result of failure to act will be loss of *periousia,* since her allies will defect and Spartan military power will in the end prove unequal to that of her adversaries. Once *that* happens, Sparta will lack the means to achieve anything (δύναμις) and her basic strength (κράτος) will have been lost forever. All five of the necessary elements will thus have disappeared. The Spartans are too trustful, claim the Corinthians, too unwilling to recognise their peril, and the Athenians trade on that lack of perception. Power properly used should express itself in action, not in a passive waiting for and acceptance of the initiative of others. It is a sentiment which von Clausewitz would have endorsed to the full. 'In such dangerous things as war', he wrote,[25] 'the errors which proceed from a spirit of benevolence are the worst'.

Fortunately for themselves, the Spartans *were* roused and they *did* take action before it was too late. But the success which alone could justify their resolve and confirm their power long eluded them. The final sanction of war, in which they were the acknowledged experts, and which was the hitherto successful foundation of their *kratos* and *dynamis,* was not invoked with the expertise traditional to Sparta and expected by allies and adversaries alike. Even when events were running strongly in their favour they failed to use them to the best effect; such is the occasion of Thucydides' observation which prefaces this chapter. For most of the war, except its last phases, events ran badly for them; what is more, they seemed to have no *tharsos* with which to face adversity and no *gnome* with which to rectify it. Sparta in the Peloponnesian War may as a result exemplify for us in Thucydides' pages not only power in relation to a military machine but the defects of such power, or rather its propensities for failing to operate successfully.

First, however, we may consider briefly what advantages the Spartans possessed in their attempt to defend their established, though potentially declining, position. These were, roughly speaking, the advantages which attend all military powers or military despots to whom their subjects owe loyalty as a matter not of affection but of self-interest. Because arms were the foundation of Spartan society and Spartan success, every attention was paid to the training and education of the young men in fitness and discipline; indeed, as we have seen, the whole existence of a Spartan was conducted in a spirit of preparedness for defence against revolt and gave him a military skill unequalled in any other *polis*. The Peloponnesian army was composed, as to its nucleus, of such dedicated men. It was filled out by allied troops who all had an interest in supporting the Spartan régime—which in no way treated them tyrannically for all that its advantage to them was primarily military. Thus the army fufilled Machiavelli's requirement for the security of a principality, that it must rely on its own arms.[26] The Corinthians observe that Athens' *dynamis* has to be purchased—Sparta's is home-grown (οἰκεία);[27] it is an important point.

The Spartan system of government provided a centralised direction and a continuity of command which were often lacking elsewhere. Spartan admirals and inferior commanders changed a good deal, perhaps so that no one in the oligarchy might get above himself; when this sort of rotation was not effectively applied, as we see in the case of Lysander, the dangers only too readily became apparent. But the kings, who regularly commanded on land, the vital element to Sparta, were hedged about with constitutional safeguards so that they could not abuse their position; *and yet* they lost nothing of the advantage which experience of command provides.

To back all this, they had a tradition of victory. For over a century before the Archidamian War broke out they had never lost a pitched battle when their full strength had been deployed—save for Thermopylae, which had redounded to their credit nonetheless. The old music-hall song expresses sentiments which a modern generation would scarcely find palatable:

> And when we say we've always won,
> And when they ask us how it's done,
> We proudly point to every one
> Of England's soldiers of the Queen.

But it was stirring, manly stuff, and the Spartan army fulfilled its sentiment to the letter. The Spartans alone of Greek armies, it appears, marched in step. Like a Scottish regiment they went into battle to the sound of the pipes, though pipes of a very different sort, and one may see the operation depicted on the François Vase. *Ésprit* was allied to training, efficiency, and traditional courage. 'Return with your shield or on it' was the Spartan mother's fond farewell to her soldier son. It was a simple maxim, but it expresses all that goes to create successful military power if properly harnessed and led. Thus Sparta appears to have fulfilled von Clausewitz's requirements of talent in command, military virtue, and national sentiment; at least, she fulfilled the requirements better than anyone else.

Since successful war is the final sanction of successful power, and the Spartans possessed all the ingredients which go to make it up, they ought to have won the Peloponnesian War fairly quickly and to have re-established their jeopardised position with little trouble. For the majority of them the *casus belli* was a straightforward, honourable, black-and-white uncomplicated issue—'have our allies been wronged or have they not?'[28] And the underlying issue, the 'truest cause', if Thucydides was correct in his diagnosis of it, was equally straightforward—were the Spartans to remain powerful and secure or not? They had every incentive to get on with the job and every expectation of finishing it in accordance with their wishes. Yet Thucydides clearly expected that Athens, not Sparta, was the more likely winner,[29] and although Sparta did win it was, we might say, almost in despite of herself. Napoleon no more than endorsed Thucydides when he said that the best general was the one who made least mistakes, and it may be that war is, in the last resort, a competition in costly errors; that side whose errors are the less costly runs out the eventual winner.[30] But such a process of attrition through mistakes tends to take time, as it did in the case of the Peloponnesian War; and even there the Spartans were saved only by the timely intervention of the Persians to underwrite their losses. What in fact happened was that the Spartans proved not to possess, or to have failed to benefit from, the advantages with which we have just credited them. If in theory Thucydides laid his bets against them, and if in practice they belied their own reputation, we might profitably enquire why.

In the first place, successful application of military power assumes its superiority over power of the same kind. The Spartans were denied the chance of fighting the pitched battle at which they excelled, for the simple reason that the Athenians would not come out and fight. When such a battle did take place the Spartans won it, as at Mantinea.

But they were sometimes compelled to fight the kind of battle for which they were not trained, as at Olpae; and their prowess at sea, on which element they had to win if they were ultimately to defeat Athens, was far outranked by that of the Athenians. They were thus unable to bring their essential *periousia* to bear.

The effect of this was unexpected to the other Greeks, for whom Spartan courage was proverbial. It was a decline of *tharsos*. When their traditional tactics, with which they knew they could win, failed them they lost heart; fortune seemed to be against them, and they were affected by what Thucydides calls ἔκπληξις μεγίστη.[31] Their fighting showed less spirit, and they began to feel that anything they undertook was foredoomed to failure. For a people of traditional bravery there was a remarkable element of fear which appeared from time to time in the Spartan character. This was the subject of an interesting if rather exaggerated article a generation ago, which nevertheless did a service in drawing attention to the point.[32] What is more, the Spartans' image abroad suffered from their failure to live up to their courageous reputation. The other Greeks were amazed when the Spartans on Sphacteria preferred to surrender rather than to die.[33] It was not until the battle of Mantinea had been fought and won that Sparta's international prestige was satisfactorily restored.[34] In the interim the Spartans had been through all the anguish of the period of the Peace of Nicias, which they had only successfully surmounted because their dissident and dissatisfied allies failed to find better accommodation elsewhere.

Part of the trouble lay with what von Clausewitz called 'methodicism'. In its way the careful following of an approved and tested method by troops well trained in carrying it out is a valuable thing. 'If we see Frederick the Great's generals always making their appearance in the so-called oblique order of battle, the generals of the French Revolution always using turning movements with a long, extended line of battle, and Bonaparte's lieutenants rushing to the attack with the bloody energy of concentrated masses, we recognise . . . that method of action can reach up to regions bordering on the highest. The evil is only that such a manner originating in a special case easily outlives itself, because it continues while circumstances imperceptibly change.'[35] The same evil had gripped the Spartans. They showed no flexibility, no ability to adapt to change and adopt new methods, let alone turn them to their advantage. Instead, they lost heart; 'loss of hope rather than loss of life is what decides the issues of war', wrote Liddell Hart,[36] and it was a dictum the truth of which the Spartans very nearly proved.

Loss of *tharsos* was accompanied by lack of *gnome,* for methodicism afflicted commanders as well as commanded. They did not know what to do when things went awry. The famous despatch after the battle of Cyzicus, reported by Xenophon, is typical and truly laconic: 'the ships are lost; Mindarus is dead; the men are starving; we do not know what to do'.[37] Since power is dynamic and must express itself in positive, thrustful action, the Spartans were from the first in the less favourable position of simply attacking in order to defend. The fact that they *had* taken the initiative in the war did not alter the validity of the overall picture, that it was Athens who had the dynamism and was on the way up. It is this conviction—that Sparta

was only making a despairing attempt to avert the inevitable
—which had impressed itself on Thucydides. Sparta thus
had no positive reserves of forceful intent—nothing like that
restless determination always to be pressing forward which
the Corinthians observed in the Athenians. 'A mere appeal
to material interest or self-preservation', says Liddell Hart
in another context, 'will never produce a dynamic effort.
For that we need a positive faith, not a negative fatalism.'[38]
Unfortunately, all that Sparta could produce, when positive
faith was required, was indeed a negative fatalism. 'L'audace, et encore de l'audace, et toujours de l'audace', cried
Danton. But the Spartans, courageous enough in battle, had
not the courage of the spirit to sustain them through long
years of adversity. The Spartans won the war, thanks to
Persia and Athens and Syracuse. They could almost be relied
upon to fail to win it for themselves; they were 'convenient
enemies', as Thucydides remarks. They had in fact neglected, because of their stereotyped approach, to observe the basic
principle which Liddell Hart described as 'a simple rule
containing the conduct of war in a nutshell'. 'What is the
outstanding principle of fighting, whether between individuals, armies or nations?' he asked himself.[39] Being
knowledgeable in such matters, he was able to provide a
succinct and exemplary answer—'It may be summed up
thus: "Pick out your opponent's weak spot and hit him there
with all possible force, whilst at the same time guarding
against the possibility that he may knock you out instead"'.
This the Spartans had not done. The Athenians had and
kept the initiative, until their self-inflicted catastrophe in
Sicily deprived them of it. It was not until 413–412 that the
Spartans were in a position to try again what they had

failed originally to do. Did they make any better attempt with their unexpected second chance?

The occupation of Decelea, an idea not their own but derived from the joint *gnome* of Alcibiades and the Corinthians, showed some readiness to adopt a new strategy, a recognition of the bankruptcy of the old.[40] And now that the maritime grip of the Athenians was loosened, especially with the expectation that the Syracusans would send them substantial assistance, they were able to take to the sea with some prospect of success. But it was not enough to have the opportunity; this they owed to fortune and to the failures of their opponents. They must make the fullest and best use of it. Their record in the period 413–411 does not encourage us to feel that their *gnome* and their *tharsos* had taken an upturn commensurate with their *periousia*. The essential of the situation was to keep the Athenians on the run, to select their most vulnerable point and 'hit them there with all possible force', giving them no chance to recover. Athens' most vulnerable point, as history was to demonstrate more than once, was the Hellespont; to this the occupation of Attica and the raising in revolt of Ionia, though desirable and contributory, were subordinate. An immediate blow in the north, disregarding if need be the other considerations, would have best served their purposes and could have shortened the war by many years. Admittedly, conflicting claims were being pressed upon them—most immediately from Chios and from the satrap Tissaphernes. These they could have afforded to pass over, if a short-term result was reasonably in prospect, as indeed it was. Pharnabazus was as ready with support as his more southerly colleague, and the prompt arrival of a Spartan-Syracusan fleet in northern waters, taking advantage of the potential revolt of Lesbos en route, could have caused Athens fatal embarrassment.

But Pharnabazus was not applied to until the Athenians recovered themselves.[41] The Hellespont and Lesbos were given low priority,[42] and when the Spartans did eventually get around to Lesbos the revolt there went off at half cock.[43] As soon as the Athenians were able to win a victory in the Hellespont, the last that Thucydides reports, at Cynossema, *their tharsos* was completely restored.[44] They had turned the corner, and the subsequent victory at Cyzicus made them feel they were well embarked on the road back. Equally at fault was the Spartan neglect of Euboea. Thucydides emphasises very markedly the importance of Euboea for an Attica under enemy occupation.[45] Agis had an opportunity to raise Euboea in revolt in late 413, and had got as far as getting two commanders and 300 hoplites up from Sparta to go over there;[46] but the Spartans tried to do too much at once, Euboea was neglected, and it was not until 411, after two years' dissipation of effort, that the island received the help it required. When this took place, the effect was electric; yet even then the Spartans neglected an even better opportunity in order to carry it through.[47]

The plain fact was that they still lacked confidence. Their newly found energy was provoked by their enemies' catastrophe and the insistence of their allies, actual or prospective. Their own approach was at best a determination to 'pull their socks up'. The sea they viewed with misgiving; circumstances had compelled them to acquire a navy— κατ᾽ ἀνάγκην ἤδη τοῦ ναυτικοῦ προσγεγενημένου.[48] They thought that if they got down to things all danger from Athens would be at an end, and their position of power (ἡγεμονία) would be reinvested with its pristine security (ἀσφάλεια).[49] Their thinking, that is to say, was still basically negative and defensive, and this we have already seen to be incompatible with the power of a military state. Here again there is a marked contrast, even at this low ebb of their fortunes, with the approach of the Athenians.[50] We may add to this an unhappy lack of rapport between Agis, commanding in Attica, and his home government.[51] Some allies applied to the one, some to the other. Sparta spoke with two hesitant voices when she should have spoken with a single clear one. This internal weakness had plagued Sparta before. In the pentekontaetea, in 432, in 421, there had been the conflicting policies of those behind who cried 'forward' and those in front who cried 'back'. It was an internal weakness of direction which went some way to creating Sparta as a state equipped to win a war but to lose the peace.

It comes back, in the end, to the fatal elements of indecision and inflexibility in the Spartan character. 'If a man behaves with patience and circumspection and the time and circumstances are such that this method is called for', said Machiavelli,[52] 'he will prosper; but if time and circumstances change he will be ruined because he does not change his policy. It is better to be impetuous than circumspect; because fortune is a woman, and therefore if she is to be submissive it is necessary to beat and coerce her. Experience shows that she is more often subdued by men who do this than by those who act coldly. Always, being a woman, she favours young men, because they are less circumspect and more ardent, and because they command her with greater audacity.' In the context of power, it was Athens that was youthful and Sparta aged; it was Athens that could command fortune, and Sparta that could not; and to that extent military power, although representing the final sanction by which all power may be maintained, is insufficient if it relies only on von Clausewitz's three postulates of skill in command, virtue, and national spirit. These requirements may win battles; they do not win wars. These are won, as Pericles emphasised,[53] by *gnome* and *periousia,* and nothing we have yet seen has served to suggest that the great man was wrong.

Chapter 6

The magnitude of the change that has taken place can best be appreciated if you read and compare the treaty with Persia which was made in the time of our hegemony, and that recently published. Formerly, as will readily be apparent, we set limits to the King's territory; we prescribed what some of his imposts were to be; we kept him from the seas. Now, however, it is he who controls the destinies of the Greeks, who dictates what each of them must do, who has practically set up his own viceroys in every city of Hellas.

Isocrates, Panegyricus 120

People who have never exercised power have all kinds of curious ideas about it. The popular notion of top leadership is a fantasy of capricious power; the top man presses a button and something happens; he gives an order as the whim strikes him, and he is obeyed. Actually, the capricious use of power is relatively rare except in some large dictatorships and some small family firms. Most leaders are hedged about by constraints—tradition, constitutional limitations, the realities of the external situation, rights and privileges of followers, the requirements of teamwork, and most of all the inexorable demands of large-scale organisation, which does not operate on capriciousness. In short, most power is wielded circumspectly.

J. W. Gardner, University 29 (1966), 10

It is no use bringing up against me the cliché about the despotic power of Xerxes going down before the liberty of the Athenians. When I refer to a larger, more total Power, I mean a Power which demands and obtains relatively more from its people. It is certain that in this respect the Power in the Greek cities over the citizens was far in excess of that of the Great King over his subjects. For instance, the Ionian cities which were subjects of the Persian monarch had only to pay him a small tribute, which was often remitted them. Apart from that, they were self-governing.

B. de Jouvenel, Le Pouvoir, 135

The Great Power

Until that day (the battle of Marathon), the very word 'Persian', when they so much as heard it, struck terror into the Greeks.

Herodotus VI 112

WHEN, from the distance of two and a half millennia, we look back with a more universal view upon the wranglings and janglings of the city-states of classical Hellas, we may be forgiven for finding them unpleasantly parochial and puny. We have continually to remind ourselves that the magnificent legacy of Hellenic civilisation gives them an importance which transcends their intrinsic narrowness and sterility. As I have suggested elsewhere,[1] the Greeks of the classical period were in a sense living on borrowed time. The period of their greatest achievements in all the available fields of endeavour of the human spirit coincided with the fortunate absence of external pressures, during which they were able to engage in the luxury of almost perpetual intra-Hellenic discord without prospect of effective interference. Had there been such a prospect, Hellas lacked the unity and the power to resist it successfully. The Greeks could hardly expect a repetition of the amazing *bouleversement* of 480, nor, when the moment of crisis came, did such a repetition take place. When the cards were on the table, as the fourth century was to show in all its decisiveness, it was the big battalions, the great nation-states, that counted—as still they do. It is worth observing even the basic point that 'the Great Powers' is the name by which these states are called. And where the world of the Greeks is concerned, only Macedon and Persia qualify to be considered for such a title.

Of the two, one may be immediately discarded. Macedon in the time of Thucydides had only potential, not yet co-ordinated and realised. When that potential *was* realised, under the skilful leadership of Philip II, the Greek *poleis* had little chance of withstanding it, whether individually or collectively. For the time being, however, the Macedonian kingdom was comparatively weak, and its coastal areas were a field for the independent activities of the *poleis* located there, as well as for the intervention of Athens and Sparta. Archelaus I (413–399) went some way towards displaying the possibilities of a powerful Macedon, but his predecessor, Perdiccas II (454–413), a good deal of whose reign was spent in combating separatism within his kingdom, showed himself an unreliable ally and an ineffective opponent to both sides in turn during the Peloponnesian War. His nuisance value was admittedly considerable, and the Macedonian theatre of war was important, but Perdiccas' Macedon was emphatically neither 'powerful' nor 'great'. It is to Persia that we must therefore turn when we seek to examine the 'Great Power' aspect of the exercise of power in Thucydides; and it so happens that in the historian's final book Persia re-emerges, after a generation of acquiescence in the verdict of the conflict of 481–449, as an important factor in the Greek political scene.

That being so, no apology is needed for beginning with a quotation from the *Panegyricus* of Isocrates, which was published in 380, nearly a quarter of a century after Athens' surrender of her *arche*. Half a dozen years before, in 386, the so-called King's Peace had been more or less imposed by Persian pressure on a chronically divided Greece. It had compelled the Athenians, along with everyone else, to accept what was a reasonable but, in the circumstances of its imposition, humiliating *modus vivendi*. The Greek cities of the coast of Asia Minor were to belong to the King, on a principle admitted by the Spartans in 412, and the remainder were to be free and autonomous. Isocrates (and he was not alone in this) saw the peace as a national disgrace[2]; the orators of the fourth century join him in pointing the contrast, as he does here, with the Peace of Callias two generations earlier—within the lifetime of some of the oldest citizens, when it was the Athenian *demos* which had dictated terms to a no-longer-so-great Great King happy to accept them and call it 'pax'. In their own day they had to face the fact that the boot was on the other foot, that Persia was an arbiter in Greek affairs in a manner inconceivable to the contemporaries of Pericles. The origin of this changed state of affairs lies to no small extent in the events recorded by Thucydides in his eighth book, and the orators turned the knife in their audience's largely self-inflicted wounds by reminding them of the better days that once had been.

Paradoxically, it was *because* Persia was basically no longer to be feared, as Cary has indicated, that her position as *tertius gaudens* in fourth-century Greece was acceptable. The King intervened in Greek affairs on a more or less equal footing; that he could do so—and did—was, considering the fifth century and its history, humiliating in itself. What added to Greek humiliation was the knowledge that there were no troops to equal Greek hoplites, that the King relied on Greek commanders and mercenaries, and that his power was in fact less at a time when the Greeks themselves gave him more scope for its exercise. The Peace of Callias had once and for all robbed Persia of its capacity to appear as a positive menace. With the Persian bogey laid, medism became respectable. The contrast between 450 and 380 points up the Greeks' own incapacities; it does not betoken any basic change in the nature of Persian power vis-à-vis its own ability to exercise itself effectively. Here the real contrast is that between 450 and 481—or 490, for which Herodotus is the eloquent witness. Then the very name of Persia inspired dread. The sentiment is echoed in Xenophanes and the Theognidea[3]; and naturally so. For the Persian Empire was the wonder of the late archaic age—a positive, dynamic power, not owing its exercise merely to the divisions and follies of those with whom it had to deal, as in the weaker Empire of the second Artaxerxes. This was the generation of Darius I, when the King's realm stretched as far towards the rising sun as Greek geography could well envisage. The Greeks could, and undoubtedly did, reflect upon the inexorable advance of Persian dominion, before which all those potentates whom they had regarded as enjoying the summit of human success and felicity had fallen, a dominion to which many of their brothers had already been forced to bow the knee. Myriads of warriors, the finest in the world, could be summoned by their lord's command or whim to a campaign destined to be crowned with inevitable victory. No obstacle could withstand such a power; the earth had to yield passage to his ships, as at Mount Athos; the sea had to yield passage to his troops, as at the Hellespont; nature herself was forced to acknowledge the triumphant majesty of the Great King. And Herodotus and Aeschylus,[4] impressed and fascinated like everyone else, communicate their own awe to us across twenty-five hundred years, as they enumerate the contingents that set out from Sardis to compel the Greeks to join the rest of the civilised world in subjection to this greatest of all great powers. At Doriscus the great army halts and is counted. Herodotus, who has dwelt on the march out from Sardis and the crossing of the Hellespont, at this point gives his long and graphic catalogue of a host which, dazed with its magnitude, he records at the last as some five and a quarter million.[5] This figure he in fact quotes when, just before the Artemisium–Thermopylae encounter, the opposing forces come for the first time into collision, and he returns yet again to the theme of the stupendous character of Persian power. And to be the commander of this enormous, overwhelming display of complete *kratos,* none was more worthy than the King himself, Xerxes.[6]

Here, in effect, is the analysis of the Great Power *par excellence.* I have dwelt on it, because I sometimes feel that its familiarity in our studies takes the edge off it for us. We know all too well what was to come. We lose sight of the feelings that animated the Greeks before that extraordinary *peripeteia,* that hundred-to-one chance, enabled Hellas to survive.[7] Beneath the legends and heroics that soon obscured the luck and muddle by which battles so often are won, the Greeks knew it was more by the King's errors than by any prowess of theirs that salvation came.[8] Our contempo-

rary sources leave us in no doubt what our feelings should
be, if we try to transport ourselves, say, to 492, before even
Marathon came to shed a welcome ray of light in the en-
veloping gloom.

A powerful, well-trained army had formed the basis of a
dynamis which had created for the founder of the empire,
Cyrus, an *arche* by a process of acquisition of *kratos*. The
ingredients, and the process, are precisely those which I
have enunciated on an earlier occasion. Abundance of territory, abundance of population, abundance of treasure, had
produced that *periousia* which we have seen to be an
indispensable concomitant of power. It was an abundance
more vast than anyone had yet known, more grandiose
than a Greek, accustomed to the more modest standards of
city-state Hellas, could well comprehend. Nor was the final
essential element lacking. The whole movement of conquest
and expansion had received its impulse, had been infused
by, the *gnome* of the two great monarchs, Cyrus and Darius.
Its territory vast, its wealth boundless, its armies invincible
in numbers and bravery, its kings shrewd and splendid—no
wonder that the Greeks of the early fifth century trembled
at the very name of Persia. The phrase is no mere literary
flourish.

The legend had been shattered by Marathon, Salamis,
Plataea, Mycale, Eurymedon and, finally, Cypriot Salamis
also. The Peace of Callias, whatever its juridical character,
had completed the process. Persia was no longer to be
feared; the King could be attacked with relative impunity;
Greek political sentiment turned, within a couple of generations, from dreading him, via harassing him, to making
use of him.[9] In 430 the Spartans sent an embassy to seek his

assistance, but this was intercepted by the Thracians and Athenians and never reached its destination.[10] In 425/4, when Darius II came to the throne, the Athenians had the good fortune to capture a Persian envoy coming to Sparta— from whose documents it appeared that a number of Spartan embassies had already taken the road to Susa, although the King had not found it easy to understand what they wanted.[11] The Athenians took the opportunity to renegotiate, as it appears, the Peace of Callias with the new monarch, in which Epilycus, uncle of the orator Andocides, was their chief ambassador to the King, with the useful mediation of one Heraclides of Clazomenae so prized as to be rewarded by the great and unusual honour of a grant of Athenian citizenship.[12] That the Athenians had already been active, even before this, in negotiations with the King for help against the Peloponnesians we may gather from the *Acharnians* of Aristophanes.[13] What is, however, remarkable is that nowhere between this point (IV, 50) and the beginning of Book VIII does Persia come into Thucydides' picture at all. To be used or ignored—that was all that Persia meant to the contemporaries of Cleon and Nicias and Brasidas.

By 412 Persia was no less wealthy or extensive than she had been. It is true that provinces revolted from time to time—usually at the instigation of a satrap related by blood or marriage to the monarch and apt to dispute his succession or challenge his fitness to hold his position. It is true that any Persian king had to safeguard himself by intrigue and frequent carnage within his court. But the vast resources and the big battalions were there still. All the same, as was emphasised in the previous chapter, there is more to the exercise and command of power than military potentiality and pecuniary resources. For Persia the essential fires had gone out. Power must be successful if it is to maintain itself; that of the Persians had been latterly unsuccessful, and decline was the inescapable consequence. That is to say, while the physical ingredients were to a considerable extent still present, the moral ingredients had gone, the *tharsos* and the *gnome* which alone could make the *dynamis* and *kratos* effective. The *gnome* of the Greeks may not always have been their strong point, but there was no doubt that, although they lacked *periousia* on the Persian scale, it was they who now had the *dynamis, kratos* and *tharsos* where a comparison with Persia was concerned.[14] Thus the 'Great Power' factors which the possession of the big battalions and the enormous wealth ought to have conferred on the Persians were not fully substantiated. Therefore, despite her size and her resources Persia ought not, in the early stages of the Peloponnesian War, to be classed as a great power. She was powerful and she was great; but there were flaws in her power and her ability to exercise it which, on a close analysis, may be held to deny her the top classification.

The weakening of the Athenian command of the Aegean, and the evident willingness on the part of the Spartans to go cap in hand for Persian subvention, made the point at which Book VIII of Thucydides begins the ideal opportunity for the King to make a comeback—to renew those dreams of Hellenic conquest which Xerxes had had perforce to abandon. Yet neither now nor later was there any idea of resuming a programme of expansion into Europe. The Persians never ceased to claim sovereignty over the Greek cities on the Ionian coast;[15] it is arguable that they had never renounced any such claims, but that for practical reasons they had not pressed them at the time of the Peace of Callias or its re-enactment when Darius II had become King.[16] The Athenians, for their part, had as it seems been content to enjoy the facts of the situation and had not sought to stir up trouble over the juridical aspects of it. Be that as it may, the untroubled possession of his Asiatic territory seems to have been the effective limit of the King's ambition in 412 and later. It was essentially a defensive policy; it contains that element of *hesychia* which, in the context of Sparta, I observed as having been stressed by the Corinthians as characteristic of the Spartan approach to the problems of their situation in 432.[17] A satisfied power, content with the *status quo,* with everything to lose by expansion and adventure, is a power in decline. Persia was already a power in decline, and her actions at this time emphasise the fact.

One may here contrast the very close and contemporary parallel of Carthage and the Greeks in the west. Carthaginian pretensions in Sicily had been shattered at the same time (some even said on the same day) as those of the Persians in Greece itself. For the next seventy years the Greeks disregarded Carthage, on the supposition that it was an extinct volcano; some are even said to have thought in terms of conquest of it.[18] But just as in 412 the stage was set for a Persian comeback in the Aegean, so in 409 the Carthaginians were able to venture on a comeback in the west. Within four years they had conquered most of Sicily and driven the powerful Syracuse, the Athens of the west, into a humiliating peace and the arms of a fierce despotism. Until Hannibal, two centuries later, abandoned his undertaking against Rome, Carthage never ceased to menace. Yet in the east, in the Aegean, such a thing did not happen. Carthage recovered her dynamism, her *dynamis,* and in consequence regained her lost *kratos.* She was no longer content with *hesychia,* with acceptance of the verdict of Himera and therefore with the acceptance of the inevitability of decline. It was the same sentiment which she displayed after her defeat by Rome in the First Punic War. Persia made no such resurgence; Alexander's victories completed a process of regression which began at Salamis and which the opportunities of 412 did nothing to halt.

Thucydides gives three different treaties between Sparta and the Persian King, drawn up when both sides had realised that Athens' weakness gave them mutual interest in mutual action.[19] Why there should be three has been a subject of much discussion, the general conclusion of which seems to be that it is the last, that given at Chapter 58 with a proper heading and dating according to the eponymous ephor at Sparta and the year of the King's reign, which is the ratified and operative version.[20] The other two may be interpreted with some plausibility as, in essence, earlier agreed drafts from which the final text was hammered out by negotiation. In these first two drafts there is a clause of wide significance: 'Whatsoever territory and cities the King holds or the forefathers of the King held, shall belong to the King' is the sentiment of the first draft; in the second it appears as 'Whatsoever territory and cities belong to King Darius or belonged to his father or their ancestors, against these shall neither the Lacedaemonians nor their allies go either for war or to do any harm; nor shall either the Lacedaemonians or their allies exact tribute from these cities'. In the first draft the thoroughgoing character of the clause—so thoroughgoing as to suggest that this is basically the draft of Persian terms for the treaty—would have surrendered to the King all the territory of mainland Greece north of the isthmus of Corinth, for King Darius' ancestors had certainly come into possession of that territory, even if they did not maintain their title to it for very long. The second version, perhaps that put forward by the Spartans in response to these exaggerated claims, is in effect a neutralisation of the territory in question; it would remove from the Great King's potential grasp not only those territories of Europe which Xerxes had conquered but also the Ionian cities which the Athenians had liberated. The final version, short and clear, is a kind of compromise between the two, but a compromise which nevertheless compelled the Spartans to appear as the betrayers of their Hellenic brethren: 'The King's territory, in so far as it lies in Asia, shall belong to the King, and concerning the territory that is his the King shall determine as he pleases'. It was a compromise with which the King was content.

With this clause the Spartans, as we know, gained deserved obloquy and much trouble for themselves; their attitude of subservience destroyed the position of strength from which, as we have seen, the Greeks had been able to operate towards Persia since 449. But although representing a kind of recovery on the King's part, the clause is in essence an admission of *hesychia,* an acknowledgement of limited aim and therefore an acquiescence in potential decay. Power which ceases to be dynamic is already going downhill. Persia could not fill the vacuum which Athens left, and neither, as it proved, could Sparta. It was Philip and the Macedonians who, in the end, obliged.

There is a little more to be said about this clause, however, and it is perhaps worth taking the present opportunity of saying it. Wade-Gery[21] drew attention to one of the clauses in that passage of Isocrates about the Peace of Callias which prefaces this chapter—'We prescribed what some of the King's imposts were to be'. Since, to judge from the Peace of Nicias,[22] autonomy and the paying of tribute were not incompatible in the Greek view, it is not unlikely that the Greek cities of Ionia did hold a double allegiance and pay a double, though moderate, set of *phoroi*—to the King for their country territory and to Athens for the territory and revenues of the *polis*. It is not mentioned by Wade-Gery that this might well be echoed in the phraseology of the second of the two draft treaties we have looked at. For the King's territory (as the final version also emphasises) was customarily known as the royal *chora* (χώρα). In the first draft the King claims the entire *chora* of his ancestors; in the second there is an attempt to neutralise both *chora* and *poleis:* that is to say, the Spartans concede the neutrality of the cities and their revenues, if the King concedes the neutrality of the *chora* that he has claimed. The final version renews the Persian claim to the whole of the *chora* in respect of Asia. It is possible that the Spartans interpreted this as not pressing a claim on the *poleis,* while the King, who had not been prepared to accept draft two, never recognised any distinction between *chora* and *polis*—or was not now intending to do so even if once he had.

An analysis of the resources of the Ionian and Aeolic cities by J. M. Cook[23] suggests that this idea of double dependence has more substance than that of a mere theory to reconcile a casual literary statement with our general tradition. Liberation by Athens had cut off many of the cities from their agricultural hinterland,[24] and archaeology indicates that the fifth century in Ionia, so far from being a flourishing period of glorious freedom, was in fact one of urban pauperisation. These cities were materially better off in the sixth and fourth centuries than they were under the Athenian Empire. 'The Peace of Callias', said Cook,[25] 'cannot have been a cause of jubilation in Ionia'; at least, one may modify, not to all Ionians. All the treaty with Sparta did was to remove this dual and ambiguous situation; and that, in the context of this argument, is the point.

The ambivalence in the situation of the Ionian cities may perhaps be reflected in the general ambivalence of the Greek attitude towards the power of Persia. That that power had once been great and fearful they well knew, and they knew that they had feared it. In any case, to imply otherwise would have been to tarnish the lustre of the great victories of 480 and 479, to which they never ceased to refer. They had learned to live with Persia, and had learned to feel that she could be disregarded as a practical danger. By 412, therefore, it had become a reasonable thing to treat with the Persians— indeed we have seen that it was reasonable at an earlier stage, though nothing came of it. Yet, in spite of all that, a stigma of a kind still remained. There is a sort of parallel, which I will not press because of the obvious differences, in the attitude of the 'Western democracies' to the Soviet Union. Until 1941, the Russians were the fearsome purveyors of red revolution, the enemies of democratic society. However, under the stress of war and with a mutual foe, alliance with them became ultimately respectable.[26] From that time on, despite a renewal of the old situation in the last years of Stalin, the attitude has gradually taken root that Russia *can* be admitted as an acceptable member of the community of nations, and that, properly watched, the hug of the red bear is not so much to be feared as an earlier generation imagined. This does not of course prevent spy scares and the resurgence from time to time of waves of anti-Russian and anti-Communist popular sentiment. Similarly, despite the new Persian respectability as an equal partner with the Greeks in diplomatic negotiations, and despite the subconscious appreciation of Persia's essential weakness, there were times when a sudden and irrational 'Persia scare' seized hold of Greek public opinion. There was such a moment in 355 when the Athenians feared a Persian expedition against them.[27] Such fears were basically unreal, but deep-seated and ingrained attitudes die hard. This is an element of power which should not, indeed, be ignored. People may take it at its face value, or more than its face value; it can live on a tradition, even though the tradition has long since ceased to bear any relation to reality. It is possible, for instance, that an irrational antagonism to Germany in Britain may long outlast German militarism and the expansive tendencies of German nationalism, simply because of the terror and slaughter that these once brought about. Equally, a readiness to appreciate the realities of the situation in the late fifth and fourth centuries, and to do a deal with the King on an equal footing, could not be entirely divorced from a deep-rooted awe and fear of Persian power; and this made the humiliation of which Isocrates is our spokesman even more unpleasant to endure.

Not, of course, that the King's power relied entirely on memories of a more glorious past. He could, and did, apply real pressure when and where it was needed. But he usually did so through the agency of someone else. His activity was diplomatic. He kept the situation in Greece satisfactory to himself by paying the Spartans to do so—that is, by underwriting their hegemony. When, in the early 380's, the Athenians were in his view beginning to overreach themselves again he was able, via the Spartans, to bring about the Peace to which Isocrates so much objected. He did his best with the cards in his hand—cards which, on the whole, the Greeks themselves had dealt him. But they were cards which were limited in their possibilities. His trump cards, the big and invincible battalions, were devalued. The lesson of Plataea had been reinforced, for the fourth-century monarchs, by Cunaxa. When Alexander invaded Asia it was a grandiose undertaking; let us make no mistake about that. But Alexander's toughest opponents in the overthrow of the power of the Persian king proved to be geography and the Greek mercenaries in the King's pay.

Thus the attitude of the Greeks towards Persia emerges as an amalgam of all sorts of contradictory elements—disdain, born of the Peace of Callias and the victories preceding it, reinforced by Xenophon and his Ten Thousand; fear, born of the age of Cyrus and the first Darius, and still rearing its ugly head from time to time; humiliation, that a power despised, feared, and yet known to be in a state of progressive weakness, should hold the balance in Greek affairs; matter-of-fact equality, that could do a deal with the King on a man-to-man basis, and could answer, for instance, the claim for assistance addressed to them by rebellious satraps in 362 by saying that they have no quarrel with the King, and if the King treats the Greeks squarely and on the level, they will treat him squarely and on the level too, that is, by not supporting a revolt against him.[28]

These attitudes, and the situation of which they are the expression, derive from the redress of the balance in the King's favour which the events of 412 brought about. The redress was, as we have seen, more apparent than real. Its cause lay partly in the destruction of Athenian hegemony and partly in the compounded development of Greco-Persian sentiment through the fifth century. But, as we have also observed, the new situation revealed the King's basic limitations. I say 'we have observed', because the size and wealth of Persia, and the lack of external pressure to hasten the process of decline, meant that that decline was not so swift or thoroughgoing as to be readily apparent. That decline had taken place the Greeks did indeed realise with, as it were, one part of their minds; but with the other part of their minds they saw a great monolithic power of inexhaustible wealth whose resources they could fear and at the same time use. They needed them. Lacking resources of their own with which to fight one another, they were delighted to find that the King was willing for them to draw upon his; and they were also delighted, though at the same time annoyed with themselves, to find that the King's price was a price that, with a hard swallow, they could pay. After all, there was much that they could admire in Persia. It was not for nothing that Xenophon, when wishing to describe the education and training of a complete gentleman, chose Cyrus, the founder of the Persian Empire, as his model. Yet, to point up the ambivalence of their approach, one must set beside that the action of King Agesilaus of Sparta during his campaign in Asia, also recorded by Xenophon,[29] when he ordered the Persian captives put on sale as slaves to be exhibited naked, so that their soft, white bodies, unused to exercise in the Greek fashion, should demonstrate to the troops that the enemy was no match for them. When all was said and done, the Persians were barbarians, and necessarily inferior to Greeks. Not only were they the slaves of the King but, as Aristotle was to define it, they were slaves by nature (φύσει δοῦλοι).[30]

I mentioned at an earlier stage that Thucydides contains no reference to Persia between the year 424, in Chapter 50 of his fourth book, and the beginning of Book VIII, when the changed situation introduced Persia as an extremely serious factor in Greek affairs. Andrewes has suggested that this omission of any treatment of Persia during twelve years represents an underestimate on Thucydides' part.[31] The historian was concerned to complete his Sicilian section, and was unable to finish either Book V or Book VIII, or indeed to revise Book IV to the extent that he might perhaps have wished. Had he done so, Andrewes suggests, he might have included more material on Persia which would have led us more intelligibly into the position suddenly presented to us in Book VIII, when Amorges the bastard son of Pissuthnes appears as in revolt against the King, supported by the Athenians. In the circumstances in which they found themselves at that time, this intervention by the Athenians is apt to strike us as gratuitous and foolhardy. Their backs were to the wall in Greece and the Aegean; now least of all could they afford to fool about in Ionia supporting the forlorn cause which is suppressed the very next time that it is mentioned.[32] It therefore seems necessary to say something about the Athenians and Amorges, and to precede that something by the suggestion that Thucydides was not necessarily in the wrong in omitting Persia from his narrative for a decade.

There had been times when some action of Persia, or of the local satrap who represented Persia to the Greeks, had been of concern to Greek affairs. There had been the possibility, which Thucydides thought fit to mention,[33] that Pissuthnes, then satrap in those parts, might have helped Alcidas at the time of the siege of Mytilene. There had been the revolt of Colophon from the Athenian Empire in 430 and the rescue of Notium in 427 from the same fate.[34] But Pissuthnes, active also in the Notian affair, had subsequently revolted from the King, probably at the change of monarch in 424/3; and this had effectively removed Persia from the Hellenic scene.[35] The Athenians had got on with winning the Archidamian War untroubled by any need to insure their eastern flank. Indeed, as long as that particular pot was kept boiling (and it may be that they should make sure it was), they could embark with clear consciences on even wider adventures, such as that in Sicily.

Pissuthnes had been active for a long time; he was already satrap in 441, at the time of the revolt of Samos.[36] If indeed he did revolt as early as 424, he maintained himself as an independent power for a further decade; if his actual revolt did not come until later, at least the early years of a new king's reign were not years of external interference, for there was too much to be attended to in the way of internal stability. At any rate, it was not until Tissaphernes, son of Hydarnes, was sent westward by the King that Pissuthnes was disposed of, and this did not happen until 413. Pissuthnes' fate did not terminate the independence of the satrapy, but it jeopardised the continuance of the revolt, and for their own safety, and that of their territories, the Athenians felt obliged to take some action. It is clear that they did not do so until it was Amorges who had inherited the revolt and Pissuthnes was no longer on the scene.[37] It was their best chance of keeping the Persians busy and giving them no opportunity to assist Sparta in 'liberating' the cities of Ionia. They were even prepared to entrust some of the cities to Amorges himself. It is apparent that Iasus, one of the cities of the Athenian Empire, was in Amorges' hands when the Peloponnesian fleet sailed along and took it by storm; and Amorges and his men were the more taken by surprise because they had assumed that the fleet they saw sailing up would be Athenian.[38] It happens that at Iasus there survive the remains of a handsome fortification on the landward side; it remained unfinished, although if it were attributed to Tissaphernes or to a later age, the dynasty of the Hecatomnids, there is no reason that can readily be seen for its being left so. G. E. Bean and J. M. Cook attribute it, with great plausibility, to Amorges, who had the wealth to embark on such an undertaking.[39] The size of the fortification, in a sense, demonstrates the magnitude and seriousness of Amorges' revolt. A considerable army would have been needed to man it, and with such an army and with the Athenian navy at his back Amorges would have been comfortably situated in an impregnable position. The history of Persia in the fourth century shows that the growing independence of breakaway satraps, who became dynasts merely acknowledging Persian suzerainty (and that not always very seriously), was one of its central features. Pissuthnes and Amorges, we may suggest, were in advance of their generation in realising the latent possibilities in this direction, and the advantages of these possibilities were not lost upon the Athenians.

But it all came to nothing. The important points which emerged were that the central authority was re-established at this crucial time, that the King and his able minister Tissaphernes were disposed to do an important deal with Sparta, and that the Athenians and Amorges were unable to establish a state of affairs in Ionia and Caria that would have been indicative for the future. Thucydides, on his regularly careful and judicious reckoning of what is relevant and important, has not undervalued any of these events. He has put their strict value on them with regard to the actual development of affairs, and isolated, as he always does, those features which proved to be of real consequence. They did not necessitate any alteration in his previous books, nor, I suspect, would he have thought with hindsight that they did, even had he lived to carry out the completion of his task.

What, finally, may we derive from our analysis of the Great Power at this juncture of Greek history? A monolith with cracks known and exploited, but still great enough to be awe-inspiring, Persia became a new factor in Greek affairs not because *she* had changed but because the Greeks had. The most effective weapon she had left was her wealth, and its use had limits; it was effective because the Greeks permitted it to be so, and they were angry both at its effectiveness and their permission. It suggests two things—that great powers are sometimes only as great as others allow them to be, and that every apparently monolithic power does in the end develop cracks. It is hard for the generation which has to wait until this happens, but it is encouraging to think that happen it will. The chief danger to the Persian monolith, the crack-producing phenomenon, partly involved the geographical factor—the difficulty of reconciling central control with local initiative *and* with local loyalty. In an age of fast transport when distance has become diminished, when sources of information are controllable and controlled, yet information itself easily disseminated, a monolithic power can create a greater security for itself, and such cracks may not appear. But, as Horace said,[40] 'Naturam expelles furca, tamen usque recurret'. We are dealing with laws of the rise and fall of power which, in the end, will find their own means of operation.

Chapter 7

If you are seen to be playing the part of liberators, the more firmly based will be your power in conducting the war.

Thucydides III 13, 7

The faculty of reason may lie relatively unused in the majority of a people, but there is not a man anywhere who is incapable of emotion. And it is to the emotions, therefore, that appeal must be made. Rouse in your behalf trust, hope and affection; rouse against your rival indignation, anger and hatred—and success is yours. It is truly complete, when a public meeting can be induced to cheer a speech which it cannot understand and greet the other side's reply with stampings of the feet.

B. de Jouvenel, Le Pouvoir, 233

All political authority rests finally on moral factors—on the trust placed in it by man.

Gerhard Ritter, The Corrupting Influence of Power, 27

(Captions to a series of nine drawings of a man dressed as a beach lifeguard)
I walk around on the beach all day—
In a pith helmet, sweat shirt, red trunks and a whistle—
So everybody thinks I'm a lifeguard—
Which I'm not:—
And any time I see some guy bigger, better-looking and more
      muscular than me making out with a girl—
I blow my whistle at him—
And I yell 'Hey you, get away from there'—
And I let him off with a tongue-lashing and a warning—
And *I* take the girl.—
*Power!**

Jules Feiffer

Power and Public Opinion

AT the very beginning of Plato's *Republic,* when the definition of δικαιοσύνη, 'justice', is first attempted, an interpretation adumbrated by Cephalus and carried further by Polemarchus is politely but swiftly disposed of by Socrates.[1] It is that right conduct consists in telling the truth and discharging one's obligations—the hallmark of the true gentleman, as we may also gather from Xenophon's account of the education of the Persian monarch Cyrus. As amended by Polemarchus, with reference to the poet Simonides, this amounts to rendering every man his due—doing good to your friends, therefore, and harm to your enemies. Socrates discounts this notion by means of a *reductio ad absurdum,* but it is to be noted that Polemarchus, though bewildered by Socrates' skill, still clings to his belief.[2] It was, after all, what he had been brought up on, a sound practical maxim reflecting the norm of civilised society, guiding day-to-day actions by a moral doctrine introduced partly to provide a general standard (so that all those among whom the same convention is shared will know how their fellows will act and react) and partly to give transient actions a more than transient validity.[3] By its means, these actions are related, through the use of value words, to the eternal verities—duty, truth, the good, the harmful. It is action according to a predictable norm and sanctified by sound moral backing which appeals to the man-in-the-street, and insofar as power is in his hands, or derived from and accountable to him, the action in which it expresses itself must conform to these requirements.

It is noticeable that in the early Platonic dialogues the first efforts to define the abstract quality selected for discussion always express themselves in terms of action. In the *Laches,* for example, courage is 'sticking to one's post in face of the enemy and not running away'.[4] In the *Charmides, sophrosyne,* which we have hitherto rendered as 'restraint' or 'moderation', is expressed as 'to do everything in an orderly manner without fuss, like walking along the street and talking and everything else'.[5] The man-in-the-street needs to have a moral reason and justification for doing what in fact he does do, or what he wants to do, even though he may not profess any high standard of morality, or indeed profess any morality based on metaphysical or religious conviction; and he will feel this need even though the actions themselves possess no inherent moral connotation—when indeed they respond, on analysis, to laws which are devoid of moral content. The concept of power, which has been the theme of these investigations, falls into this category; in itself, it has been envisaged as independent of morality. But that is not the attitude towards it which is generally accepted and generally acted upon. Public opinion has a different approach towards it, concerning which two points must first be made. This first is, that its proper use follows almost exactly Polemarchus' definition of justice; the popular attitude to power is that you use it to help your friends and do down your enemies, and that in so doing its use must be endorsed by the term 'just'. The second point—and one which has been postulated at earlier stages of the discussion —is that power is popularly held to express itself in positive action, in achieving the individual end that you want to achieve.

On this second matter the quotation from Jules Feiffer, which precedes this chapter, is eloquent enough. The definition is of that Platonic kind we have just looked at—'power is chasing off the rival and getting the girl'. It is evident that to the ordinary man charity very properly begins at home, and number one comes first. Plato's analogy in the *Republic* between the microcosm of the individual man and the macrocosm of the *polis* is exact, in that states operate their policies on the same premisses as those on which the individual citizen operates his. The principal use of power is to promote our own advantage, ὠφελία, and our honour, status, or dignity, τιμή, by helping our friends and among them our best friend, ego; and it is further used to ward off apprehension, δέος, by harming our adversaries who arouse feelings of apprehension in us. To this extent, therefore, the evidence of Thucydides which we have considered in this connexion accurately produces what we may judge to have been the current, everyday approach to communal or individual action. Where we run into difficulty is that Thucydides in his analysis of the matter is strict in discounting the basic validity of our first point—that you use it, to help or harm, in a manner regarded as 'just'. To him all arguments revolve, when the cards are on the table, around the requirements of expediency and advantage, and we have seen that this is a fair assessment since the power intending to achieve these things is not in itself concerned with any other aspect of the matter. Nevertheless there remains a need for spiritual or moral support, a need to say that an action is 'right', that a decision is 'equitable', that shares are 'fair', that a war is 'just' or even 'holy', that an inquisition is *ad maiorem Dei gloriam,* that chicanery, slaughter, destruction are carried out for ends which are in themselves 'good' on an absolute standard (thus of course 'justifying' the means) and which bring benefit to their victims even though the victims may not, at least in this world, be able to testify to the accuracy of this appraisal. You can make a desert, as Tacitus later observed, and call it 'peace';[6] you can give it, indeed, any name you like, and it will be valid for you with all its overtones. Whatever the *Realpolitik* behind the action, the necessity of giving it a respectable nomenclature cannot be gainsaid.

These last remarks, as it happens, have dwelt particularly on action involving pain, but we may equally consider action involving pleasure. There is a puritanical streak in mankind which worries over enjoying things. Extreme Puritans denounce all pleasure as sinful; if you enjoy anything, it must be bad per se. So it is necessary that whatever is pleasant, ἡδύ, must also be pronounced good, ἀγαθόν. Even a relativistic philosopher like Protagoras, whose most famous dictum proclaimed man's right to set his own standards, was prepared to maintain that. 'To live pleasurably is good and to live unpleasurably is bad, don't you agree?' said Socrates to him. 'I agree', replied Protagoras, 'but on the assumption that the pleasure consists in the enjoyment of τὰ καλά, honourable things'.[7]

The second generation of sophists, as we know, were prepared to go a stage further than that and dispense with any provisos containing ὀνόματα καλά, 'fine names' which cloak reality. In so doing, like the Athenian negotiators at Melos, they showed a frankness and honesty in acknowledging openly what previous generations, more respectable but more hypocritical, had been unwilling to admit, although Thucydides reveals that the basic factors were equally operative throughout the events with which he deals. Justice involved your τιμή, ὠφελία, and δέος; that was a fact of life, and there was no need to dress it up in camouflage. It was the name you gave to successful power in action. This is not, however, an attitude confined to the generation of the *sophistai:* it remained true for the next generation and the next, and has remained true ever since. Pearson quotes in this sort of connexion a passage from Demosthenes' speech *On the Freedom of the Rhodians,*[8] and it is so apposite that it is worth while to do the same in the present context:—'I think indeed that it is just for you to restore the Rhodian democracy; but even if it were not just, when I look at what these people are doing, I still think that I should urge you to do so. Why? Because, men of Athens, when everyone is anxious to do the "just" thing, it would be shameful that you alone should refrain. But when all are in fact making such preparations that they will be able to act in defiance of justice, for you to hold back, taking shelter under the skirts of "Justice" I hold to be not a just act but an act of cowardice. The fact is that every man measures "justice" with an eye on the actual powers that he possesses'. We may compare that final sentiment with what the Athenians say in the Melian Dialogue—'You Melians should try to get what it is possible for you to get, taking into consideration what both of us really do think; for you know as well as we do that, when these matters are discussed by practical people, "just" is a word to use in evaluating men's actions when external limitations operate equally on both parties.'[9] The lesson is as valid for the conflict of the mid-1960's in Vietnam or for the World Wars of the twentieth century, as it was for Athens and Melos then.[10]

Successful power creates its own history and its own philosophy. Sir Ronald Syme, in his classic work *The Roman Revolution,* constructs his interpretation of the career of Emperor Augustus on that thesis, but without making any selection in the ancient world, Orwell's *Animal Farm* can exemplify the point effectively enough. We have seen that the political actions of the Athenian *demos,* of the aristocrats and of individuals, all obeyed the rules of power in the absolute sense, without moral connotations. But although Thucydides rightly, as we noted, strips from his assessment of motive the moral trappings which do not belong there, morality keeps on creeping back. People want it there, and think either that, despite what the 'realists' say, it is indeed there—or, if it is not, then that it ought to be. Pearson suggests that ordinary men and women are not disposed to think in terms of ideals.[11] On the contrary, I believe firmly that they are—especially the young ones who have not yet been obliged to accommodate them to what life actually has to offer. They feel great hesitancy in acknowledging that the bases of public conduct are without moral connotation, that is, *a*moral. They mistake *a*morality for *im*morality, and naturally assume that this is discreditable, that the moral standards of individual private conduct ought to extend to the conduct of public and international affairs from the standpoint of the state as a whole. 'What rascals we should be', Cavour is reported to have said, 'if we did for ourselves what we do for our country'. The standards are in practice not the same, whatever in theory they ought to be, and this produces a personal dilemma presenting itself to many an individual as a conflict between patriotic duty on the one side and the misgivings of conscience on the other, which is so widely and keenly felt when people are called upon by their government to support, and perhaps to die for, a cause they regard as of dubious merit and questionable justice. There arises, as a result, a tendency to obscure the point that laws of power are involved which are completely neutral to this inward struggle of the human spirit. Public opinion thus introduces a moral element and finds moral problems in the context of the exercise of power, and this has a necessary effect on our evaluation of Thucydides' standpoint. In consequence, the extreme realism of the historian may in some instances and to some extent require to be modified. In expressing so uncompromising a thesis he may be misrepresenting the actual situation. Since people act by what they believe to be so, rather than by what is so, action is often prompted by moral considerations which may be a deceptive mask for, or indeed in conflict with, considerations of real advantage. Such moral considerations may have no real connexion at all with the action in hand. Modern parallels are not hard to seek, and there is no need to dwell on them; they make it additionally evident that the need to be assured of moral righteousness oneself, and to take a holier-than-thou attitude with those who do not share the same convictions, is deep-seated in humankind.

This intervention of morality in public opinion, and its modification of the exercise of power, is usefully illustrated by Thucydides by means of an inconsistency in his third book. It was contended earlier, in connexion with the Melian Dialogue, that on Thucydides' argument the

Athenians' springs of action are close to those of which Callicles and Thrasymachus in Plato's *Gorgias* and *Republic* would approve.[12] But it was also noted that that particular interpretation of power is the one least likely to be used, let alone acknowledged, by a truly popular government. Popular opinion is more emotional and sentimental, and tends to be diverted from a strict reckoning of policy on the realistic basis of expediency by the introduction of what people consider to be humane and moral factors. Thucydides himself gives the impression that he disapproves of the line of argument he attributes to the Athenian negotiators at Melos, finding it logically compelling but objectionable when put into practice. At least, we receive such an impression from him, and hypotheses on the character and plan of his *History* have been built upon it.[13] It may be suggested that it is an impression which we perhaps derive to some extent from his exposition because we want to derive it. For we would not willingly believe that Athenian democrats could have expressed their policy and beliefs in terms of such cynical realism. Thucydides refuses to obfuscate the plain issues. We may suspect that in reality the Athenian negotiators did obfuscate them,[14] for that is what people generally do, and it is what we ourselves prefer should be done. Thucydides will have none of it. Time and again in his *History* he causes the specious pretexts and pretences in which realities are customarily shrouded to be discarded by speakers aiming to reveal in all its nakedness the absolute truth of the matter, τὸ ἀληθὲς τοῦ πράγματος. He might, like Protagoras, have found some virtue in the theory of the social contract and in the belief that the general morality in affairs which most people follow is a reasonable guide which should not be rejected. Socrates made a gallant but lonely attempt actually to equate justice with expediency, insisting that a man would come to realise that to act on the basis of *arete* (ἀρετή, 'virtue'), was his most profitable course if only he could be brought to a knowledge of that in which true *arete* consists. Lack of that knowledge mars his assessment. If true *arete* is beyond his attainment, at least a 'true opinion', an ὀρθὴ δόξα, of its nature and what it involves is possible for him; to acquire it, his faculty of assessing (if the 'technique of measurement', the μετρητικὴ τέχνη, in the *Protagoras* represents the general trend of Socrates' own ideas in this respect) needs to be educated. But Thucydides keeps 'moral' words distinct from τὸ ξυμφέρον, 'expediency', as (we may judge) did most modern intellectuals of his generation. It was for popular consumption, and by the people themselves, that the distinction was blurred. To the extent that Thucydides discards this 'blurring', therefore, he may fail to present an accurate portrayal of the situation with which he is dealing. If a man's life is essentially founded upon innocent falsehood, it is not correctly delineated or explained by an analysis of the truth.

The example from Book III of Thucydides just referred to is concerned with the Mytilenaean debate. The arguments adduced in that debate by Cleon and Diodotus are intellectual arguments exclusively concerned with a relative assessment of *to xympheron*—what decision will be most in Athens' real interests.[15] We may notice in passing that, speaking as he is before the *demos,* Cleon speaks in terms of the ἀδικία, 'injustice' or 'wrongdoing', of the Mytilenaeans; Mytilene has done gratuitous harm to Athens, and it is expedient for the Athenians to punish her for it. Diod-

otus will not argue about the *adikia,* but disagrees on the
expediency of the punishment advocated by Cleon. However, the preliminary to this renewed debate, which was a
second assembly gathered to review and possibly revise the
decisions of the first, shows that the reason for its being held
had nothing whatever to do with expediency or even with
the fact of *adikia* which was admitted. The grounds were
entirely humanitarian: 'people began to think how cruel
and how unprecedented such a decision had been—to
destroy not only the guilty but the entire population of a
state'.[16] Of this, in the debate itself as recorded by Thucydides, there is nothing.[17] A brief introductory remark by
Cleon, that where rebellion is concerned compassion has no
place, serves only to highlight its absence in the rest of the
discussion. But Thucydides does record it as having motivated people, and one may suggest that for the purposes of
his exposition of what really mattered he allows Cleon to
brush it aside all too swiftly, even though Cleon does so with
all the adroitness one would expect of him.[18] For this motive
was, in the context, of major importance, and those in
power or seeking power must always reckon with it as a
factor of motivation.

It is of course a useful reason to insert by way of an extra
argument, to help to justify a man's doing what he had
intended to do in any case. For instance, Phrynichus suggests in 411 B.C. that the Great King will prefer to ally himself with Sparta rather than with Athens because in the past
the Spartans have done less harm to Persia than have the
Athenians; on that account Phrynichus is prepared to place
the less confidence in Alcibiades' hopes of getting Persian
help for Athens.[19] Basically, however, the King is not

regarded by Phrynichus or anybody else as shaping his imperial policy on a real desire to repay a benefit. Lionel Pearson[20] sees this remark as a significant allusion to a belief that relations between states may be guided by such wishes; but it is a significance which I cannot see. It is one more reason, thrown in by Phrynichus on the basis of the average man's view of *arete,* for not trusting Alcibiades. The King would adopt the course of action that was likely to show the most advantage to Persia. He might, indeed, quote a desire to repay Sparta's benevolence as an ostensible reason for doing what he thought was most advantageous to him; he would obviously not trouble to quote it unless he thought that such a reason mattered to someone and he felt that it would cut some ice with them. The evident fact was that it *would* matter to someone—that people do want and look for reasons of this kind, because considerations of expediency by themselves have an appearance of immorality and the ordinary person does not care to be seen to be associated with them, however much he really is. He acts, as nature and the facts of power bid him, in a manner which will best redound to his personal advantage, but he imposes a stigma on the word 'selfish', and wishes to pretend that his motivation was other than it actually was. He invents formulas to satisfy his conscience, or demands that these be created for his consumption.

Similar considerations entered into a good deal of what has been said about the Athenian aristocrats and their plans for revolution, that something was required which was, in Thucydides' words, εὐπρεπὲς πρὸς τοὺς πλείους, 'plausible and fine-seeming for popular requirements'.[21] As a modern parallel we may observe the manner in which political trials are managed in Communist countries. It is clearly expedient that those who have opposed or offended the régime, and therefore, *ex hypothesi,* the common good, should be put out of the way. This goes without saying as part of the philosophy, and needs no argument or apology. Yet immense trouble is taken to bring them before a properly constituted court, to obtain their self-denunciation as having transgressed against the interests of the people, and to go through all the machinery of official justice. Everyone knows from the start what the outcome must be, and why it must be. But so much trouble would not be taken unless those in authority needed to convince people at home and abroad, and perhaps also to convince themselves, that what they were doing was 'just' in a popularly acceptable sense, and that they had morality and not merely expediency on their side.[22]

That such considerations might be ignored at their peril may be usefully illustrated from the career of Alcibiades, and to this fascinating character it is profitable on this occasion to devote a little more attention. Our historical detail about Alcibiades, as it emerges from the pages of Thucydides, does not allow us to entertain the idea that anyone who really thought about the matter was under any illusions about him. Thucydides himself, who may (as we saw) have known Alcibiades personally rather well, had no illusions when it came to an evaluation of his actions. 'Alcibiades seems then for the first time to have rendered a service to his country inferior to that of no man', he says of him at the time when Alcibiades restrained the Athenians at Samos from sailing back to the Piraeus to unseat the Oligarchs.[23] In his speech to the *demos* early in Book VI

Alcibiades dwells at length upon his personal fitness to command on the score of his genuine services to the state.[24] But Thucydides states facts as he sees them and does not endorse Alcibiades' claim. Nothing that Alcibiades had been concerned with hitherto had, in the long run, been to Athens' advantage. It is important to emphasise that morality is in no way involved in this appraisal; nor, I believe, is there any criticism of Alcibiades' essential ability. It is a plain statement of the practical results of that ability.

Nor is Phrynichus under any illusions about Alcibiades either. 'The general opinion (of those working for the oligarchy)', writes Thucydides,[25] 'was that they could have confidence in Alcibiades' plans; but Phrynichus entirely disagreed with them. He believed, quite correctly, that oligarchy and democracy were all one to Alcibiades and that what he was really after was to get himself recalled by his friends, and come back to Athens as the result of a change in the existing constitution'. Finally, Alcibiades was not, I have already suggested, under any illusions about himself, and never had been. But he knew the need to sell himself to a *demos* that needed illusions, under a general smokescreen of what was plausible and sounded good. The *demos* did not have to be Athenian; the same laws that we have investigated held good for *demoi* anywhere, and Alcibiades' speech at Sparta shows him at his best in handling them.[26] This speech is a masterpiece and deserves a more careful analysis than is here in point. Pearson remarks that 'the hybristic arrogance of his argument is breathtaking, but it is not based on considerations of expediency, as one might expect from a pupil of the sophists. It is rather a perversion of the theory of justice based on friendship'.[27] However, in my opinion Pearson has not looked hard enough at the context, which Thucydides, in framing Alcibiades' speech, has accurately reflected. Alcibiades here expresses what may be described as τὰ δέοντα, the essentials of the case, with remarkable judgement and skill. It is *because* it is a perversion of the theory of justice based on friendship that it is truly sophistic, and it is *because* he uses the argument as he does in these particular circumstances that it is, for him, truly expedient.

For Alcibiades well knew that a popular audience, be it Spartan or Athenian, must have its ὀνόματα καλά, its fine phrases and polite names for things. Perhaps the fact of his exile reinforced that knowledge, which he had previously neglected to his cost. Where there is illusion, there can also be disillusion, which is a dangerous phenomenon for those liable to be held responsible. It had been Alcibiades' lack of *sophrosyne,* his neglect of what people might think of his conduct, which was, I suggested, his undoing in 415.[28] However much he might despise public opinion, he had to take it seriously if he were to survive and prosper as a statesman; he did not take it seriously enough, and this in itself constitutes a major and lasting criticism of his genuine statesmanship. He went part of the way; he had glamour and flamboyance, and he played to the gallery in *that* sense. Beyond that, however, he omitted to put himself to the necessary trouble, and so gave offence. In 415 there were, as a result, too many people ready to believe the worst of him, and too many more ready to be talked into such a belief. Alcibiades was selfish, as most people are; unlike most people, he did not bother to try seriously to appear otherwise. That this was a moral defect I am not concerned to argue. It was, more importantly, a violation of the laws of power which worked to his detriment, for his honour, *time,* and his advantage, *ōphelia,* suffered in consequence.

This is perhaps a useful opportunity to return to a consideration, which in the context of the discussion about him was not fully explored, of Alcibiades' lack of patriotism; this always provides a major stumbling-block in any modern attempt at an assessment of him.[29] I claimed at the time that no moral issue was involved; but there certainly was a political issue, and it arose because of the moral delinquency attached to Alcibiades' unpatriotic desertion to the other side. We may contrast Socrates' determination to obey the laws of the city, even when they did not suit his personal convenience. Frederick the Great said that honour and the interests of the state were his two guiding principles. For him, fortunately, the two were or could be made identical. But Alcibiades, in whose eyes a similar identification appears to have existed, could not be his own interpreter in the matter as Frederick was. Alcibiades' action, in consequence, got in the way of the whole of the future relationship between himself and his city. This is mentioned simply as a practical effect upon practical affairs. Once again it does not detract from Alcibiades' essential abilities or nullify his undoubted gifts. But it mattered, and it still matters, and it illustrates very clearly that the intervention of moral judgements must be held to matter even by those to whom they mean nothing. There is for us an additional hazard in that we may, in our assessment of him, introduce standards which were alien to him. That is to say, if we condemn him as 'unpatriotic', are we not liable to do so on the basis of a standard of 'patriotism' manufactured by ourselves to which he was not himself prepared to subscribe or which indeed he would not have recognised?[30] Nonetheless people do make judgements, on the standards acceptable to themselves, and, in our present case it is Alcibiades who suffers so that they may feel comfortable.

Because people in general are open to emotional appeals on the grounds of humanitarian and moral principles, it might seem that a clever politician can always have it his own way, if he has an eye on *to xympheron* (particularly his own) and if he has a knowledge of collective behaviour. But this is not so; the people can always get their own back. To maintain itself, power must show success after success, and these successes are attributable not to the politician who engineered them but to the *demos* who selected him. Public opinion, in short, is always right and always claims the credit where there is any credit. But in case of failure, it is not the people who erred; it is all the fault of the politicians who misled them and the public servants who betrayed their trust.[31] Popular opinion is very much concerned with responsibility, and is only ready to acknowledge its own responsibility when there is some advantage in it. The Sicilian expedition is an excellent case in point. Had the Athenians conquered Syracuse, the glory would have been the glory of the victorious *demos*. But it ended in disaster, and, as Thucydides is quick to observe, when the news sank in 'they turned against the politicians who had been in favour of the expedition, as though they themselves had not voted for it, and also became angry with the prophets and soothsayers and all who, at the time, by various methods of divination, had encouraged them to think that they would conquer Sicily'.[32] In a crisis, in any state of alarm or bewilderment, when things go wrong, when there are developments the ordinary man cannot assess or understand, public opinion looks for a scapegoat. There must be something, or someone, to blame, and to impute blame is an inescapable necessity. The people themselves cannot have made the mistake. To cry *peccavi* is the most difficult thing the ordinary human spirit can do. When it is done we are very ready to believe it either explicable only on the basis of an excess of genuine religious inspiration and humility or ascribable to the efficient and practised methods of Communist or Fascist gaolers, according to the circumstances in which we learn of it.

A predominant impulse in the search for a scapegoat is to blame a hostile deity. Thucydides relates how in 430 B.C. the Athenians did that very thing, when the calamity of the Great Plague struck them and they died like flies from it;[33] for they remembered that Apollo, god of healing as well as god of the Delphic oracle, had promised the Spartans, when before the war began they consulted his shrine, that he would come to their assistance whether they specially asked him to do or no. Apollo, therefore, had fulfilled his promise and struck his blow for his Spartan allies. But the historian will have none of this. The gods play no part in his history save in that men put them there, that certain human actions are undertaken in the belief that the gods exist.[34] Because the assumption of their existence underlies the responses of men to circumstances, they are relevant; but not otherwise. Thucydides' description of the plague is justly famous as an attempt at accurate analysis of the disease itself and of what men did because of its onset. Among all the other elements of his exposition, he is alive to the point that they at once sought a scapegoat—Apollo; but he also observes that 'prayers in the sanctuaries and appeals to oracles and so forth were all alike futile; and in the end people were so overcome by their sufferings that they gave them up and paid no more attention to such things'.[35]

The next popular cry for a scapegoat—that fate is to be blamed, that fate is against one—is as little to Thucydides' taste as the fastening of the blame upon the gods. The preceding generation, if Herodotus and Sophocles may represent it, looked to a necessity higher than Zeus himself which divinely orders what shall be; and to its dispositions men must accommodate themselves with what equability of mind they can muster. Thucydides will have none of this either—at least, not in those terms. It is not his view that man is wholly master of his fate and captain of his soul, nor was the human *psyche,* in his eyes, unconquerable— any more than there were gods to thank for it. For him there was indeed a necessity, ἀνάγκη, but it was the necessity of consequence. Men choose, and certain effects must follow from the choice.[36] The compulsion can to some extent be controlled by the man of *gnome,* judgement, and wisely used since his choice will also have been wise in the first place; but even he is not fully in control. For he is subject, for instance, to the laws of power, and these too are governed by *ananke.* Men are required by a natural necessity, said the Athenians at Melos, to obey those laws.[37] And even a Pericles, wise though he might be in his use of them, and farsighted in his awareness of them, could not but be subject to them along with everyone else.

If the popular scapegoats of gods and fate do not content

him, Thucydides is at one with the generality of mankind on the third possibility—'luck', *tyche*. The role of fortune in Thucydides' *History* is an important one, to which scholars have not been slow to draw attention,[38] although they have at times been inclined to underestimate it. Pericles was fully cognizant of its hazards, and tried to arm the people against it by strengthening their confidence, their *tharsos*. 'The spirit is cowed by that which is sudden and unexpected, and which happens contrary to all calculation', he observed, 'but you are citizens of a great city, brought up in traditions commensurate with her greatness. It is therefore your duty not to flinch before disasters, whatever their magnitude.'[39] That which happens contrary to expectation and calculation, τὸ παράλογον, is a factor in history which Thucydides does not and cannot deny. The theme recurs repeatedly in his pages, and as a factor it has a highly important influence on the course of the war.[40] In this context—for this is not the place to embark upon the troubled waters of a study of Historical Causation in Thucydides or of Historicism in general—what matters is to note not only that 'luck' does have this effect of giving a twist to events and so to the course of history, and that Thucydides acknowledges as much, but that people generally think it does, and that Thucydides takes account of that too. The twist imparted by 'luck' may be nullified or its consequences mitigated by resolution, and to that extent man may still have a measure of control, as in the case of *ananke*.[41] He is neither the pawn of rational powers nor the plaything of irrational ones. But those men of Periclean calibre who can exercise such control are few. Most, when adversity comes, are able only to rail in their impotence that luck, like fate and the gods, has ceased to smile on them. One must, as the Spartans warned the Athenians, make the best of good fortune while it is on one's own side.[42] Like the rainbow, it comes and goes, beyond the capacity of the ordinary run of mankind to set bounds to its caprices.

It is easiest, best, and much the most popular to turn from such supernatural scapegoats, before whom man is resourceless, to the scapegoat readily available and easily identifiable, on whom a real and tangible revenge can be visited. The demand of the people that the guilty be hounded down and forced to purge their guilt with appropriate penalties is its most powerful and terrible weapon, greatly to be feared by anyone in the public eye. For a search is made not only among those directly concerned in the calamity which has provoked the witch-hunt, though these are as it were the primary targets. Those who are thought to be concerned, who might plausibly be concerned or by a long stretch of the imagination implicated, or even those so notorious that, though not involved in this event, they have attracted censure and ill-will on other grounds—all these may be dragged in. There is no need for Alcibiades to have been guilty of the profanation of the Mysteries. The true verdict is in a sense academic. He was needed as the scapegoat, and was an eminently suitable candidate for the role. As such he does not stand alone in Thucydides' *History*. Antiphon we have already considered, and he played the part in his turn. There are others in the Peloponnesian War—Cleophon, the generals at Arginusae, even Pericles himself. It is an element of power which, in any state save a repressive dictatorship, can have violent and unpredictable consequences. Dictatorships, it should be added, also need and use scapegoats, but theirs is a controlled and directed use, and the consequences, though they may be equally violent, are predictable and predicted. A modern analysis of a modern instance of scapegoatism is almost Thucydidean in its impact and its illumination, and will serve to illustrate the strength and irrationality of the popular forces it represents.

On the night of Saturday, 28 November 1942, there was the usual large number of customers in the club in Boston, Massachusetts, very popular at the time, called the Coconut Grove. One of the customers, for reasons best known to himself, removed an electric light bulb to make a shadowy corner a little more shadowy. This was noticed, and an attendant was sent to replace the bulb. Because he could not see very well what he was doing, the attendant lit a match; the match ignited some of the club's décor, and very soon the place was well on fire. In the ensuing alarm and panic no fewer than 488 people lost their lives. So terrible a disaster, not unnaturally, aroused public opinion. People assumed that there had been violations of fire and safety regulations; the first scapegoat was the attendant who lit the match, the next the man who removed the bulb in the first place; but public indignation soon moved on from these primary scapegoats to a condemnation of the fire department, of the owners of the club (who were said to have bribed City Hall to certify as safe an unsafe building), and of the city administration for bribery and culpable negligence. The outcry in the papers encouraged people to think in clichés and 'tabloid terms'. Phrases such as 'widespread corruption', 'crooked politics', 'underworld bosses', and the like began to fill their columns. Ultimately the alleged breaking of regulations ceased to matter; other

passions were excited, and what might have become a
serious outburst of anti-Semitism was only just averted. As
the sociologists who studied the case soon after the event
pointed out,[43] 'The people felt some person or persons must
be held responsible; attaching responsibility to mere laws
or to the panic in the club provided neither sufficient outlet
for their emotions nor opportunity for punishment. This
personalization is the rule in scapegoating'. Ever since I
first read this story I have thought how admirably Thucydides might have dealt with it. This short account of it no
more than reflects what would have been his dispassionate
brevity; but he might well have made use of it for an exposition of the reactions of popular emotion under the stress
of war which would, as we can imagine, have concurred in
the highest degree with the aims as well as the style of his
History. In so using it he would have shown that the
phenomenon of the hostile outburst tends to make any seat
of power an especially hot seat—as indeed, more than once
in recounting the events of his own times, he has the opportunity of doing. The truth of this is not the least of the
lessons that he transmits to us.

I emphasise 'transmits to us', because this brings up our
final, and most vital, question—one which refers to all that
we have investigated so far. For we must at last be brought
to enquire what there is in all this for us. Ultimately we
must recognise, on the basis of our long analysis, that it is
our own honour, or τιμή, and our own advantage, our
ὠφελία, as well as the objects of our own apprehensions,
δέος, that form our principal concern. Where does our
salvation lie, in the sense of putting the most into, and

getting the most out of, the life into which we have been thrust? We cannot contract out of such an inquiry, and we cannot contract out of an answer, much though we might like to do both and hard though many try. At the time of our birth we joined the onward march of history. It is a march of inexorable progress. 'He hath sounded forth the trumpet that shall never call retreat', wrote Julia Ward Howe, and it is a trumpet that has summoned each of us to press on, in company with the advancing multitude.

It is a condition of our participation in the march that we cannot see the way in which we are marching. We can only look backwards, and observe when, how, and in what direction our predecessors marched. That is all we have to go on as a help for our own footsteps. I cannot see how history can be viewed as a study without utility. It has the greatest utility of any study. It is our principal teacher, and although we may not heed its lessons and although we may ignore the content of its doctrines whether moral or practical, nevertheless it is the experience of others which alone can guide us in coming to grips with what we ourselves are destined to experience. The kinds of things we have been discussing, so far from being academic or remote, are in the highest degree practical and modern. The experiences of Pericles and Alcibiades were not nullified or bereft of their consequence when Pericles and Alcibiades dropped out of that historical line of march which we have since joined. We suffer with the fifth-century Greeks, and we rejoice with them, because their sufferings and their joys are in essence our own, and as such are therefore of supreme importance to us.

Some years ago, my wife and I found ourselves at that small, rural spot in the State of Virginia called Appomattox Court House. There is no need to explain what happened there 103 years ago, nor to describe its significance. A visit to Appomattox is no unusual thing for an American citizen, perhaps; but for a European it is sufficiently rare to be especially memorable and noteworthy, and the memory of it has remained particularly vivid. It was on an April afternoon, not unlike that of Palm Sunday 1865, with the sun casting long shadows and the air still, that we were there. As it happened, we were the only visitors, and had the place to ourselves. In this fortunate isolation, and being not unprepared with the proper historical background, we did not find it difficult to people the scene with the figures of a century ago—Lee tall, erect, dignified, immaculately dressed, the Virginian aristocrat in defeat; Grant mudspattered, in a private soldier's uniform with his insignia of rank roughly tacked on, courteous in a rugged but circumspect way. And all present, on both sides, conscious that they were witnessing the close of one tremendous chapter of history and the opening of another.

From somewhere in the distant neighbourhood, perhaps from Appomattox itself, there came the sound of a church or chapel bell, a single repeated note that served, in the complete quiet of the surroundings, to underline the solemnity of these reflections; as though the bell were tolling across the years for all those men great and small, good and bad, gathered at the same place on that Sunday long ago, whose ghosts the scene had conjured up. But at that instant, in one of those rare flashes of true revelation, John Donne's well-remembered sentiment came to my mind with a new dimension which it has never since lost—'And therefore send not to know for whom the bell tolls: it tolls for thee'. It is this, I then recognised as I recognise still, that makes the work of Thucydides the possession for all time that he claimed it would be. It is this, and nothing else, which is the principal lesson of history.

Abbreviations

Notes

Index

Abbreviations

AJP	*American Journal of Philology*
BSA	*Annual of the British School of Archaeology at Athens*
CJ	*Classical Journal*
Cl. Phil.	*Classical Philology*
Cl. Rev.	*Classical Review*
CW	*Classical Weekly* (after 1957 *Classical World*)
Gymnasium	*Gymnasium, Zeitschrift für Kultur der antike und humanistische Bildung*
Historia	*Historia, Zeitschrift für alte Geschichte*
HSCP	*Harvard Studies in Classical Philology*
IG	*Inscriptiones Graecae*
JHS	*Journal of Hellenic Studies*
JRS	*Journal of Roman Studies*
Proc. Camb. Phil. Soc.	*Proceedings of the Cambridge Philological Society*
REG	*Revue des Études Grecques*
Rh. Mus.	*Rheinisches Museum für Philologie*
SEG	*Supplementum Epigraphicum Graecum*
Studii Clasice	*Societatea de Studii Clasice din Rep. Populare Romîne: Studii Clasice*
TAPA	*Transactions of the American Philological Association*
ZSS	*Zeitschrift der Savigny-Stiftung, Romanistische Abteilung*

Notes

I have attempted no comprehensive and unified bibliography to accompany these pages. For one thing, the literature about Thucydides is enormous and, to quote P. A. Brunt's heartfelt lament (*Cl. Rev*. NS XVII 1967, 278)—with which one may amply sympathise, 'of analyses of him there is apparently no end'. In any case, there is little point in elaborating a long record of Thucydidean scholarship which would inevitably be incomplete and which would include, for the sake of inclusion, works not directly apposite to the theme of this book. Secondly, an ostentatious catalogue of names and works, listed (one may often suspect) partly to advertise the author's claim to omnivorous reading, can be as frightening to some as it is impressive to others.

I have therefore judged it more useful to the reader to list, at the head of the notes to each chapter, those books and articles which I found particularly helpful when I was thinking about the issues involved—although it must be understood that their relevance may not be confined to those chapters alone with which they are here specially associated. Other works are referred to in the context of the notes themselves, as occasion demands. It is very probable that I have failed to include a number of items which some may think more, or additionally, valuable: and the acute critic, I do not doubt, will discern that I have not read much that he may think I ought to have read. In any event, the views here expressed have been evolved over a long period on the basis of much reading which it would be impossible now to disentangle and reduce to bibliographic form.

Most books on Thucydides, including those which I have cited, contain their bibliographies, and for recent work on him the summaries by F. M. Wassermann (*CW* L 1956–57, 65–70, 89–101), Mortimer Chambers (*CW* LVII 1963–64, 6–14), and G. T. Griffith (*Fifty Years (and Twelve) of Classical Scholarship*—ed. M. Platnauer (1968), 188–92, 229–32) are much to be recommended. By the courtesy of the author and of the Cambridge University Press I was able to read H. D. Westlake's *Individuals in Thucydides* (1968) before its publication. H.–P. Stahl's *Thukydides: Die Stellung des Menschen im geschichtlichen Prozess* (1966) came to my attention too late for it to be taken into account in the text; but it contains much of relevance to what is under discussion here, and it has a useful bibliography. I owe it to the kindness of Professor H. Hommel that I was able to consult Renate Reimer-Klaas' dissertation (Tübingen, 1959) *Macht und Recht bei Thukydides*. But there must come a time when the reading has to stop, and when one begins to write. That time duly came, and *quod scripsi, scripsi*.

NOTE TO INTRODUCTION

1. Mme. J. de Romilly has very properly warned that Thucydides may be overpraised on this score, and that universal laws and rules for foreseeing the future may be mistakenly derived from a method which 's'accordait particulièrement avec les habitudes d'Athènes à la fin du Vme siècle' (*Fondation Hardt—Entretiens* IV [1958], 66; cf. 39–81). Nevertheless, Thucydides' insights have proved and continue to prove too illuminating for his assimilation to current needs to be eschewed. It should not be attempted uncritically, but it remains important, and indeed compelling, to attempt it.

CHAPTER 1: POWER AND THE HISTORIAN

The following books and articles will be found especially useful in connexion with the material of this chapter.

Sir Frank Adcock. *Thucydides and his History* (1963).

J. H. Finley. *Thucydides* (1947).

J. de Romilly. *Thucydide et l'impérialisme athénien* (1947; English trans. 1963).

ead. *Histoire et raison chez Thucydide* (1956).

F. Kiechle. 'Ursprung und Wirkung der machtpolitischen Theorien im Geschichtswerk des Thukydides', *Gymnasium* LXX 1963, 289–312.

M. F. McGregor. 'The politics of the historian Thucydides', *Phoenix* X 1956, 93–102.

L. Pearson. 'Thucydides as reporter and critic', *TAPA* LXXVIII 1947, 37–60.

J. de Romilly. 'L'optimisme de Thucydide et le jugement de l'historien sur Périclès (Thuc. II 65)', *REG* LXXVIII 1965, 557–75.

Sir Ernest Barker. *Greek Political Theory*, 3rd ed. (1947).

David Grene. *Greek Political Theory* (1965). Published in 1950 under the title *Man in his Pride*.

D. Kagan. *The Great Dialogue* (1965).

T. A. Sinclair. *A History of Greek Political Thought* (1951).

J. Bowle. *Hobbes and His Critics* (1951)

M. M. Goldsmith. *Hobbes's Science of Politics* (1966).

G. P. Gooch. *Politics and Morals* (Merttens Lecture, 1935).

F. C. Hood. *The Divine Politics of Thomas Hobbes* (1964).

R. M. MacIver. *Leviathan and the People* (1940).

M. Oakeshott. 'The Moral Life in the writings of Thomas Hobbes', in *Rationalism in Politics* (1962), pp. 248–300.

K. Reinhardt. 'Thukydides und Machiavelli', in *Von Werken und Formen* (1948), pp. 237–84.

H. Warrender. *The Political Philosophy of Hobbes* (1957).

Martin Wight. 'Western values in international relations', in *Diplomatic Investigations,* ed. H. Butterfield and M. Wight (1966), pp. 89–131.

F. L. Windolph. *Leviathan and Natural Law* (1951).

NOTES TO CHAPTER 1

1. Thuc. V 84–113.
2. Barker, *Greek Political Theory* 74.
3. Brown, *Hobbes Studies* (1965), ix.
4. L. Strauss, *Thoughts on Machiavelli* (1958), 292.

5. Thuc. VIII 97, 2.

6. G. E. M. de Ste Croix, 'The character of the Athenian Empire', *Historia* III 1954–55, 1–41; D. W. Bradeen, 'The popularity of the Athenian Empire', *ibid.* IX 1960, 257–69; H. W. Pleket, 'Thasos and the popularity of the Athenian Empire', *ibid.* XII 1963, 70–77; T. J. Quinn, 'Thucydides and the unpopularity of the Athenian Empire', *ibid.* XIII 1964, 257–66.

7. Thuc. VII 57, 3–4.

8. Thuc. II 8, 5; VIII 2, 2. See *ibid.* I 76, 1, where the Athenians at Sparta, in the speech Thucydides sets in their mouths, are frank in admitting the unpopularity he alleges, and Ar. *Eq.* 1111–14, Plut. *Per.* 12.

9. Lucas, *Principles of Politics* (1966), 72–78.

10. See in particular A. W. Gomme, *More Essays in Greek History and Literature* (1962), 92–101 (=*JHS* LXXI 1951, 70–74).

11. A. G. Woodhead, *Mnemosyne* (ser. IV) XIII 1960, 296–97.

12. Thuc. IV 17–22. This point was well emphasised by J. de Romilly, *Thucydide et l'impérialisme athénien* (1947), 149–55, who was at pains to justify Thucydides' one-sided exposition of the issues.

13. Thuc. I 76, 4.

14. On this see particularly F. Raab, *The English Face of Machiavelli* (1964), and on Hobbes, J. Bowle, *Hobbes and His Critics.* The aim was to make sure that, as Burke said, 'the principles of true politics are those of morality enlarged' (cf. C. Parkin, *The Moral Basis of Burke's Political Thought* (1956), 1). There is a striking modernity in the remark by W. Lucy, *Examinations, Censures and Confutations of Divers Errors in the two first chapters of Mr. Hobbes his Leviathan* (1656), sig. A, 3b, who complains of 'the genius that governs this age, in which all learning, with religion, hath suffered a change, and men are apt to entertain new opinions in any science, although for the worse—of which sort are Mr. Hobbes his writings'. See also Chapter 7 below.

15. *Leviathan* XII; *De Cive* XV 7.

16. Thuc. I 9. On the importance of thalassocracy, as emphasised by Thucydides here, see J. H. Finley, *Thucydides,* 89–91. Not to use χάρις in exercising it was, however, unwise. Cf. n. 26 below.

17. Thuc. I 11.

18. *Ibid.* 23, 6.

19. There is an equal pride reflected in an author of very different character—Aristophanes. Cf. *Vespae* 707.

20. Thuc. II 63, 2; cf. I 76, 1.

21. See Edmund Burke, *Letter to a Member of the National Assembly:* 'Those who have been once intoxicated with power, and have derived any kind of emolument from it, even though but for one year, can never willingly abandon it.'

22. Thuc. I 73–74.

23. *Ibid.* 76, 2.

24. See A. A. Rogow and H. D. Lasswell, *Power, Corruption and Rectitude* (1963), whose inquiry into the famous dictum leads them to state 'Rectitude does not vary with power. Power does not necessarily lead to corruption or to ennoblement. The connection between rectitude and power depends upon context, upon various factor-combinations in personality and society. Our inquiry has established a substantial basis in fact for the proposition that the method of thinking that found expression in Lord Acton's aphorism is fundamentally invalid' (65).

25. Thuc. II 63, 1.

26. Thuc. I 76, 3. We may note the stress laid by the Corcyreans (I 33, 2) on the goodwill (χάρις) arising from the employment of power on behalf of a friend who has been wronged. Cf. R. Reimer-Klaas, *Macht und Recht bei Thukydides* (unpub. diss. 1959), 18–19. The accession of ἰσχύς and δύναμις, recognised as the predominant consideration, is accompanied as a bonus by the χάρις of those benefitting from the proffered assistance and by the reputation for ἀρετή among the generality of people which the benefactors will acquire. Of all this, ἀσφάλεια and κόσμος are the result.

The Corinthians in their reply concede that the real policy of the Athenians must be to make their δύναμις ἐχυρωτέρα (I 42, 4), but they recommend that the best way to achieve this is by τὸ μὴ ἀδικεῖν τοὺς ὁμοίους rather than by opting for κίνδυνοι and τὸ πλέον ἔχειν. To earn χάρις, and through it ἀσφάλεια, by good works was indeed an element of Pericles' policy, and the Corcyrean argument would no doubt attract him; cf. Thuc. II 40, 4, and Chapter 2 note 70 below. The 'democrats', in whose eyes ἰσχυς and δύναμις were equally paramount, preferred on the whole τὸ πλέον ἔχειν and were not particularly concerned with χάρις. 'Ασφάλεια was too negative a concept for a dynamic policy, or, at least, ought not to be overstressed as an element in it.

27. *Leviathan* XV. Cf. M. M. Goldsmith, *Hobbes' Science of Politics,* 79–82; see also M. Oakeshott, in *Rationalism in Politics,* 289–93.

28. Cf. Thuc. I 77, 2; III 44, 4.

29. Hexter, *Studies in the Renaissance* IV 1957, 134. He continues 'Right is not might; might is not right. Might is might, and that is what *Il Principe* is about'. See also R. Reimer-Klaas, *Macht und Recht* (n. 26), 51–60, 81.

30. *Thucydides,* tr. B. Jowett, abridged with introduction by P. A. Brunt (1963), Introd. xxxi–xxxii.

31. See Barker, *Greek Political Theory,* 72–73.

32. See especially Thuc. II 36.

33. G. P. Gooch, *Politics and Morals,* 18.

34. Strauss, *Thoughts on Machiavelli* (1958), 292.

35. Thuc. II 63, 2.

36. Thuc. I 76, 2–4.

37. Although there are those who are, nonetheless, convinced that he did. Cf. P. A. Brunt, *Thucydides,* Introd. (n. 30), xxxi.

38. J. Ferguson, *Moral Values in the Ancient World* (1958), 120, refers to 'Thucydides' caustic pages' in his account of the Corcyrean stasis—'the more caustic because of their objectivity'. I feel no confidence that they are in fact either caustic or objective.

It is evident however that most people would prefer to find them so. It is held, for instance, that the *stasis* represents a special watershed in the process of Greek degeneration. So Helen North writes (*Sophrosyne: Self-Knowledge and Self-Restraint in Greek Literature* [1966], 108): 'A third stage in the deterioration of Hellas is marked by the account of the revolution in Corcyra'. But this supposition will not bear examination. Had earlier civil strife in Greece, of which there had been plenty, been less productive of savagery? The passage is no more than descriptive of what does happen in *staseis* (as it always has and presumably as it always will), and Thucydides introduces it as the first instance of *stasis* during the war, typifying its phenomena in other occurences, in accordance with a practice he adopts in other recurrent issues (see A. G. Woodhead, *Mnemosyne*, 297–98 n. 3). We cannot, or do not wish to, doubt that Thucydides disapproved of such happenings, as we do ourselves; but this is beside the point.

39. Thuc. V 89.

40. Cf. L. Tasolambros, 'Thucydides I 71', Πλάτων XVII 1965, 246–59.

41. See Gooch, *Politics and Morals*, 14, 23.

42. John Plamenatz, 'Mr. Warrender's Hobbes', *Hobbes Studies*, ed. K. C. Brown (1965), 74.

CHAPTER 2: POWER AND THE PEOPLE

The following books and articles, other than those referred to at the head of the notes to Chapter 1, were of particular use in the writing of this chapter.

A. W. H. Adkins. *Merit and Responsibility: A Study in Greek Values* (1960).

G. Grossmann. *Politische Schlagwörter aus der Zeit des Peloponnesischen Krieges* (1950).

A. H. M. Jones. 'The Athenian Democracy and its critics', in *Athenian Democracy* (1957), 41–72 (= *Cambridge Historical Journal* IX 1953, 1–26).

B. de Jouvenel. *Power: the Natural History of its Growth*, Eng. ed. (1948).

Gerhard Ritter. *The Corrupting Influence of Power*, Eng. ed. (1952).

Graham Wallas. *Human Nature in Politics*, 4th ed. (1948).

V. Ehrenberg. 'Polypragmosyne: a study in Greek politics', *JHS* LXVII 1947, 46–67.

M. I Finley. 'Athenian Demagogues', *Past and Present*, no. 21 (1962), 3–23.

H. Strasburger. 'Thukydides und die politische Selbstdarstellung der Athener', *Hermes* LXXXVI 1958, 17–40.

B. X. de Wet. 'Periclean imperial policy and the Mytilenean debate', *Acta Classica* VI 1963, 106–24.

See also A. G. Woodhead, 'Thucydides' portrait of Cleon', *Mnemosyne* (ser. IV) XIII 1960, 289–317.

NOTES TO CHAPTER 2

1. Her. V 97.

2. See D. Grene, *Greek Political Theory* (1965), 41; D. Kagan, *The Great Dialogue* (1965), 106–111.

3. *Rep.* VIII 562–63.

4. Thuc. VI 54, 5.

5. *Ibid.* 89, 6.

6. *Ibid.* 35, 2. On the sentiments expressed see A. H. M. Jones, *Athenian Democracy*, 54–55. On the 'introduction' of Athenagoras see G. T. Griffith, *Proc. Camb. Phil. Soc.* n.s. VII 1961, 21–33.

7. Kagan, *The Great Dialogue,* 76 sqq.

8. Thuc. II 37, 1.

9. Her. V 92 a, 1.

10. Ar. *Eq.* 40–49.

11. [Xen.], Ἀθ. Πολ. I 1. This matter is more fully dealt with in Chapter 3 below.

12. M. F. McGregor, *Phoenix* X 1956, 102.

13. Thuc. II 65, 7–13. See A. W. Gomme, *A Historical Commentary on Thucydides* II (1956), 190–96; A. H. M. Jones, *Athenian Democracy,* 63–65; A. G. Woodhead, *Mnemosyne* XIII 1960, 290–95; M. F. McGregor, *Phoenix* X (1956), 100.

14. The use of οἱ δυνατοί for 'powerful' or 'influential' men (or even 'the upper classes'—see Thuc. II 65, 2) is a natural and significant development from the meaning of δυνατός with reference to a man's physical strength. The δυνατοί are able to bring about effective action in their public interventions, which the small man (ἀδύνατος) cannot. See Plato, *Gorgias* 483d, where Callicles observes that it is 'just' for the better man to fare better than the man of inferior quality, and the more influential than the less influential: δίκαιόν ἐστι τὸν ἀμείνω τοῦ χείρονος πλέον ἔχειν καὶ τὸν δυνατώτερον τοῦ ἀδυνατωτέρου.

See in this connexion the apposite remark of C. Morris (*Western Political Thought* I [1967], 25): 'Willingness to face facts made the Greeks face one fact of major political importance—the inequality of man. Even when the Greeks admitted that justice meant giving everyone his due they did not necessarily mean that an equal amount was due to all; they were prepared at times to work on the principle of 'to him that hath'.' This is certainly Aristotle's view (*Pol.* 1282b), and the view of the 'best people' (see Chapter 3), although little to modern taste.

15. To act in accordance with δέος, τιμή, and ὠφελία in fact constitutes action on the basis of Machiavellian *ragioni di stato,* where *lo stato,* for Machiavelli, is not or not necessarily the body politic. Rather is it, as J. H. Hexter describes (*Studies in the Renaissance* IV 1957, 134), 'the mechanism which the Prince uses to get what he wants'. See Hanna H. Gray, in *The Responsibility of Power: Historical Essays in Honor of Hajo Holborn* (1967), 51: '[Power] becomes effective power in the political world through the Prince's art and action'.

Thucydides, however, suggests—and Callicles implies—that such a mechanism operates in the course of nature and does not have to be consciously brought into play by the Prince. Because he is what he is, the Prince will always act on the principles described.

16. Thuc. I 77, 3.

17. Thuc. III 37, 1–2. See below, pp. 157–58.

18. Adcock, *Thucydides and His History* (1963), 52.

19. Thuc. III 36, 4. See further below pp. 159–60.

20. See Theodore H. White, *The Making of the President 1964* (1965), 217.

21. On *dynamis* in Thucydides see also M. A. Levi, *La Parola del Passato* VII 1952, 81–90.

22. Thuc. I 10, 1–3.

23. For this and the next few statements, which are combined for convenience into one note, see Thuc. I 15, 1; 17; 33, 2; 42, 4; 93, 3–4; 77.

24. P. J. Fliess, in *Thucydides and the Politics of Bipolarity* (1966), 94, observes that 'no alternatives to imperialism were seriously proposed in the discussions of the Athenians'. This was not

however caused, as he suggests (95), by the 'rationale of bipolarism.' It was a natural response, requiring no explanation, and Machiavelli would have found it so. See Hanna H. Gray, *Responsibility of Power* (n. 15 above), 38: '[To Machiavelli] the acquisition, preservation and extension [of power] in a world where politics was all appeared to need no justification. The question of responsibility as accountability seemed not to require asking or answering.'

Hermocrates the Syracusan, often considered the most Periclean character next to Pericles in Thucydides' pages (see H. D. Westlake, *Bulletin of the John Rylands Library, Manchester,* XLI 1958–59, 239–68) expressly states that Athens' imperial ambitions are fully pardonable, and the grounds for this πολλὴ ξυγγνώμη are precisely those of the human and divine law which the Athenians stated at Melos. See R. Reimer-Klaas, *Macht und Recht bei Thukydides* (unpubl. diss. 1959), 48.

25. Thuc. II 62, 2–3.

26. *Ibid.* 14.

27. E.–A. Bétant, *Lexicon Thucydideum* (1843), *ad loc.*

28. Thuc. VI 18, 3.

29. Thuc. III 103, 1.

30. Thuc. II 8, 4–5.

31. Thuc. I 123, 1–2.

32. Cf. Arist. *Pol.* 1274a; A. E. Raubitschek, *Wiener Studien* LXXI 1958, 112–15 (with further references); A. G. Woodhead, *Historia* XVI 1967, 131. The connexion between democracy and seapower was indeed, as emphasised by Raubitschek, part of the *antidemokratisches Staatsdenken* of the fourth century; but it was historically justified, nevertheless, and Theopompus, who particularly stressed it, followed Thucydides' lead, as Raubitschek correctly notes.

33. 'Αθ. Πολ. 22, 3; 25, 1.

34. Thuc. I 70, 4–9.

35. The point has been well analysed by J. de Romilly, *Thucydide et l'impérialisme athénien* (1947), 151–53, to whose study it is sufficient, in this context, to refer for further detail.

36. Thuc. III 82, 6 and 8; 84, 1.

37. See A. W. H. Adkins, *Merit and Responsibility*, 235.

38. Plato, *Gorgias* 483c (see n. 14 above), *Rep.* I 344a. On *isonomia* see below p. 194 note 26.

39. See V. Ehrenberg, *JHS* LXVII 1947, 46–67. Helen North, in *Sophrosyne: Self-Knowledge and Self-Restraint in Greek Literature* (1966), 107, observes of *polypragmosyne* that 'in civic life it remains an invidious term and is so used by most writers of the fourth century'. It seems more likely that its association with the fifth-century democracy and the failure of that democracy to maintain itself and its empire in the Peloponnesian War imparted an unfavourable meaning to it for the next generations. The development of the term *phoros* and its avoidance in the fourth-century Athenian confederacy affords a parallel. See M. F. McGregor, *Athenian Policy, at Home and Abroad* (Lectures in Memory of Louise Taft Semple), 2nd ser., 1967, 22.

40. Thuc. VI 87, 3.

41. Cf. Thuc. I 76, 2.

42. Thuc. III 84, 1; cf. I 84, 1; VIII 64, 5.

43. On *sophrosyne* see further below pp. 152 and 209 n. 5.

44. Cf. T. G. Tuckey, *Plato's 'Charmides'* (1951), 5–17; R. Reimer-Klaas, *Macht und Recht* (see n. 24 above), 27–28.

45. Thuc. IV 28, 5; cf. ἀριστοκρατία σώφρων in III 82, 8. On the passage in Book IV see A. G. Woodhead, *Mnemosyne* (ser. IV) XIII 1960, 313–14.

46. Thuc. III 40, 2.

47. Thuc. I 76, 4. See Barry M. Goldwater, *Why not Victory?* (1962), 48–49: 'Many of these policies [in foreign relations] are frankly acknowledged by their proponents to be contrary to the immediate interest of the United States; yet they must be pursued, we are told, because of the overriding importance of having the world think well of us. . . .What does the world admire anyway? Strength, courage and ingenuity! . . .The very admiration and respect we covet is denied to us the moment we go out and beg for it.'

48. References in D. Kagan, *The Great Dialogue*, 41–42.

49. Thuc. I 138, 3.

50. *Ibid.* 8, 3.
51. Thuc. II 13, 2.
52. *Ibid.* 13, 3.
53. Thuc. III 45, 5.
54. Thuc. VI 24, 3. Ἐλπίς, according to Pericles (Thuc. II 62, 5), may be the enemy of γνώμη, but if it is based on γνώμη it can be the latter's useful ally. See R. Reimer-Klaas, *Macht und Recht,* 101.
55. Plut. *Per.* 20.
56. Thuc. I 18, 1.
57. Finley, *Thucydides* (1947), 92–93.
58. Thuc. II 65, 5; cf. IV 81, 2.
59. Thuc. III 42, 1; cf. 84, 1.
60. Cf. Thuc. VI 11, 6.
61. Thuc. V 14, 1–2.
62. Thuc. II 65, 9; cf. II 13, 6; 59, 3.
63. *Ibid.* 65, 3–4.
64. *Ibid.* 59, 1; IV 106, 1.
65. Cf. A. G. Woodhead, *Mnemosyne* (n. 45 above), 294–95.
66. Plut. *Per.* 16.
67. Thuc. II 65, 8. McGregor, *Phoenix* X 1956, 100, significantly refers to 'the state under Perikles, which we, unlike Thucydides, call democracy'. I wonder if we, or all of us, really would. *De jure* we might so describe it, as Thucydides did (λόγῳ μέν). France under de Gaulle could equally be called a democracy in this sense, but this did not prevent it being regarded by many Frenchmen and Francophiles as ὑπὸ τοῦ πρώτου ἀνδρὸς ἀρχή—the *de facto* situation which had saved the country from the weak and unstable democracy of the Fourth Republic. There is much in Gaullism which is indicative for the Thucydidean view of Pericleanism, for it must be stressed that for Thucydides the undemocratic elements in Pericleanism were its virtues, and that it is Pericles' mastery of the *demos* of which he approves. Pericles the Olympian, from his Athenian home or his Attic estates, like Charles de Gaulle in the Élysée Palace or at Colombey-les-deux-églises, κατεῖχε τὸ πλῆθος and μετρίως ἡγεῖτο— phrases in which every word has its full value and significance. Ἐλευθερία and μετριότης are thus revealed as the gifts of the 'benevolent despot' rather than as features inherent in the constitution, even

though the position of Pericles (again like that of de Gaulle) ultimately depended on the vote of the people. To Thucydides, of course, the particular virtue of such μετριότης and ἡγεμονία was that it was productive of ἀσφάλεια and φυλακή: and here again, in stressing the defensive and negative in Pericles' policy, he gives a distorted picture of it. See G. Grossmann, *Politische Schlagwörter* cited above, 143–44.

68. Plut. *Per.* 21.

69. Thuc. I 70, 4; 120, 3.

70. Thuc. II 63, 2. The ἀπράγμων is, in other contexts, to be characterised as σώφρων, and in circles where σωφροσύνη was an ideal ἀπραγμοσύνη went with it. See Ar. *Nub.* 1006–7, *Ranae* 727–33. The definition of σωφροσύνη advanced by Critias (Plato *Charmides* 161b), τὸ τὰ αὑτοῦ πράττειν, is certainly at variance with τὸ πολλὰ πράττειν, i.e., πολυπραγμοσύνη. The ἀρετή of the Athenians, as described by Pericles, expresses itself in actively doing good to others (δρῶντες εὖ κτώμεθα τοὺς φίλους—Thuc. II 40, 4). Ἀπράγμων ἡσυχία is characteristic of the Spartans when contrasted with the Athenians (I 70, 8), and it is King Archidamus, expressly described as σώφρων καὶ ξυνετός, who reiterates that the Spartans should consider their future actions καθ' ἡσυχίαν. It was apparently typical of him; see Plut. *Moralia* 219a (Archidamus 6), where the relevant remark is erroneously attributed to Archidamus III. For the Corcyreans such σωφροσύνη had turned out to be ἀβουλία (I 32, 4). See R. Reimer-Klaas, 27–28, and especially G. Grossmann, (see n. 67 above), 126–37.

71. Thuc. VIII 8, 4.

72. *Ibid.* 27, 3.

73. See below p. 64.

74. See Sir Basil Liddell Hart, *Thoughts on War* (1944), 58, 176.

75. SEG XII 87, XVIII 12 (with other references).

CHAPTER 3: POWER AND THE ÉLITE

The following books and articles are of general relevance to the material discussed in this chapter:

H. Frisch. *The Constitution of the Athenians,* Eng. ed. (1942).

A. Fuks. *The Ancestral Constitution* (1953).

C. Hignett. *A History of the Athenian Constitution* (1952).

L. van der Ploeg. *Theramenes en zijn tijd* (1948).

F. Sartori. *La Crisi del 411 A.C. nell' Athenaion Politeia di Aristotele* (1951).

id. *Le Eterie nella vita politica Ateniese del VI e V Secolo A.C.* (1957).

A. Fuks. 'The Old Oligarch', *Scripta Hierosolymitana* I, 1954, 21–35.

A. W. Gomme. 'The Old Oligarch', *Athenian Studies Presented to W. S. Ferguson* (*HSCP* Suppl. vol. I, 1940), 211–245 (now republished in *More Essays in Greek History and Literature*).

M. Lang. 'The Revolution of the Four Hundred', *AJP* LXIX 1948, 272–89.

ead. 'Revolution of the 400: chronology and constitutions', *AJP* LXXXVIII 1967, 176–87.

A. G. Woodhead. 'Peisander', *AJP* LXXV 1954, 131–46.

A. E. Raubitschek, Review of F. Sartori, *Le Eterie* (see above), *AJP* LXXX 1959, 81–88.

NOTES TO CHAPTER 3

1. Plato, *Protag.* 319b–323a, *Gorgias* 455b–459b. Cf. A. H. M. Jones, *Athenian Democracy* (1957), 46–47.

2. Plato, *Rep.* 520a–521b. See Liddell Hart, *Thoughts on War* (1944), 18.

3. See Barker, *Greek Political Theory*, 201–204. On the aristocracy of birth, wealth or merit see Arist. *Pol.* 1317b.

4. *Ev. Matt.* X 21–22.

5. In his demonstration that ἀρετή is not teachable (*Meno* 93a–94e) Plato may appear to controvert such a presumption by selecting a series of eminent statesmen and observing their failure to produce sons as eminent as themselves. But although the philosopher's examples are politicians, they are adduced as representative 'good men', and his argument is concerned with 'virtue' and 'goodness' in general, not with political abilities as such.

No man necessarily passes to his son his own talents or his own interests, but the son grows up in the environment in which those talents and interests are exercised and he responds to them. The history of many a family which by tradition has devoted itself to the public service suffices to make it an acceptable supposition that 'preparedness and ability to govern' may indeed be transmitted from one generation to another. Equally, there are frequent examples of medical families or nautical families or legal families in which the younger generation inherits the professional inclinations and skills of its predecessors.

6. J. M. Barrie, *The Admirable Crichton,* Act I.

7. Most succinctly expressed, perhaps, in the little verse that will be familiar to many readers—

> And this is good old Boston,
> The home of the bean and the cod,
> Where the Lowells talk to the Cabots,
> And the Cabots talk only to God.
>
> J. C. Bossidy, *On the Aristocracy of Harvard.*

8. Sir William S. Gilbert, *The Pirates of Penzance,* Act II.

9. Theognis 43–60. See A. R. Burn, *The Lyric Age of Greece* (1960), 247–57; D. Kagan, *The Great Dialogue* (1965), 33–43.

10. [Xen.] ’Aθ. Πολ. III 8. The impression of lengthy and bitter experience of Periclean democracy seems to me to argue against the contention of G. W. Bowersock, *HSCP* LXXI 1966, 33–38, that the Old Oligarch's tract is to be dated *ca.* 443 B.C.

11. *Ibid.* I 1, III 1.

12. *Ibid.* III 9, II 10.

13. Arist. ’Aθ. Πολ. 28, 1–3. The 'technical terms' used by the Old Oligarch are paralleled by those put into the mouth of Callicles by Plato (*Gorgias* 491b–c). Plato has chosen them for what they are, but if they are accurately attributable to the sort of person whom Callicles represents, Callicles' vehemence comes from the heart also.

14. See A. W. H. Adkins, *Merit and Responsibility* (1960), 197.

15. [Xen.] ’Aθ. Πολ. I 5.

16. Thuc. VIII 47, 2.

17. [Xen.] ’Aθ. Πολ. I 1, 9, III 10.

18. *Ibid.* I 10.

19. By the γραφὴ ὕβρεως: cf. Aeschines I 15; E. Ruschenbusch, *ZSS* LXXXII 1965, 302–9.

20. [Xen.] 'Αθ. Πολ. II 20.

21. *Ibid*. I 5. With reference to ἀταξία cf. Thucydides' significant use of its opposite, in verbal form, at VIII 1: 'Because the prospect on all sides was terrifying, the *demos* acted as *demoi* usually do in such circumstances and were prepared to behave themselves'—πάντα τε πρὸς τὸ παραχρῆμα περιδέες, ὅπερ φιλεῖ δῆμος ποιεῖν, ἑτοῖμοι ἦσαν εὐτακτεῖν.

22. [Xen.], 'Αθ. Πολ. I 7.

23. *Ibid*. I 8. On the equation ἀριστοκρατία→εὐνομία see G. Grossmann, *Politische Schlagwörter aus der Zeit des Peloponnesischen Krieges* (1950), 33–38.

24. *Ibid*. I 9.

25. G. E. M. de Ste Croix, *Historia* III 1954/5, 1–41. For the controversy provoked by this article see note 6 to Chapter 1 above.

26. On *Isonomia* see especially G. Vlastos, in *Isonomia: Studien zur Gleichheitsvorstellung im griechischen Denken* (ed. J. Mau and E. G. Schmidt, 1964), 1–35, with references to earlier studies. For its product, *isegoria,* see G. T. Griffith, *Ancient Society and Institutions—Studies Presented to Victor Ehrenberg on his 75th Birthday* (1966), 115–38; A. G. Woodhead, *Historia* XVI 1967, 129–40.

27. Plut. *Cimon* 15.

28. Arist. 'Αθ. Πολ. 29, 3.

29. On the oligarchic opposition under Thucydides see H. D. Meyer, *Historia* XVI 1967, 141–54, with references to earlier literature; F. J. Frost, *Historia* XIII 1964, 385–99. On the well-to-do Athenians who 'went along with' the democracy see [Xen.] 'Αθ. Πολ. II 20; C. Morris, *Western Political Thought* I (1967), 34.

30. Thuc. I 107, 6.

31. J. M. Barrie, *Courage (Address as Rector of the University of St. Andrew's,* 3 May 1922).

32. See A. Fuks, *The Ancestral Constitution,* 3–5. One may indeed speak for convenience of the 'Theramenean group', but we should perhaps beware of identifying Theramenes, as Fuks appears to do, too closely with moderate principles. It seems more likely that he

was adroit enough to appreciate that his future safety lay in his moving, at the crucial juncture, in a more moderate direction, rather than that he was an exponent of the principles his 'group' undoubtedly represented. Thucydides, although not expressing himself with complete clarity in the matter, seems to wish us to believe that Theramenes was as self-seeking as the rest (VIII 89, 3). Van der Ploeg, in the useful study cited above, gives him the most sympathetic consideration, but admits in the end that ambition was his chief motivation and that no attempt at justifying him can make of him what he was not and could not be, 'a true son of the noble community which had produced him' (269).

33. Thuc. VIII 53, 1; 65, 3.

34. See L. Van der Ploeg, *Theramenes,* 18–72; M. Cary, *JHS* LXXII 1952, 57–58. The two constitutions in the Aristotelian 'Aθ. Πολ. were not themselves, however, the unfulfilled programmes of party theorists or pamphleteers which Aristotle was somehow induced to accept as historical fact, or which had been erroneously inserted into the documentary material on which he drew. I accept the contention most recently upheld by Mabel Lang, "The Revolution of the Four Hundred" (cited above), that they represent actual documents actually enacted into law. That they were evidently preserved as enactments of the *demos* among the archives, from which we may suppose Aristotle or his source to have derived them, lends additional support to arguments for their historicity.

35. Thuc. VIII 66, 1.

36. E. Burke, *Speech at a County Meeting of Buckinghamshire,* 1784.

37. Thuc. VIII 66, 2–5.

38. See A. G. Woodhead, *AJP* LXXV 1954, 131–46.

39. Thuc. VIII 66, 5.

40. *Ibid.* 65, 2.

41. *Ibid.* 66, 1.

42. *Ibid.* 2.

43. Thuc. III 82, 4-8.

44. *Absalom and Achitophel,* pt. I, ll.83–84.

45. Thuc. VIII 67, 2–3.

46. *Ibid.* 68, 4.
47. See C. Hignett, *History of the Athenian Constitution,* 269 n. 9.
48. Thuc. VIII 68, 1.

CHAPTER 4: POWER AND THE INDIVIDUAL

Still the most useful work on the career of Alcibiades as a whole is
J. Hatzfeld. *Alcibiade,* 2nd ed. (1951).
See also
F. Taeger. *Alkibiades* (1943);
and with particular reference to Alcibiades as a source of Thucydides' material
E. Delebecque. *Thucydide et Alcibiade* (1965).
Thucydides' characterisation of Alcibiades is especially treated in
H. D. Westlake. *Individuals in Thucydides* (1968).
Among the numerous articles devoted to Alcibiades and his personality in the pages of Thucydides see in particular
P. A. Brunt. 'Thucydides and Alcibiades', *REG* LXV 1952, 59–96;
M. F. McGregor. 'The genius of Alcibiades', *Phoenix* XIX 1965, 27–46.
For Alcibiades' alleged pretensions to tyranny see
H. Berve. *Die Tyrannis bei den Griechen* I (1967), 208–10;
A. E. Raubitschek. 'The case against Alcibiades (Andocides IV)', *TAPA* LXXIX 1948, 191–210;
R. Seager. 'Alcibiades and the charge of aiming at tyranny', *Historia* XVI 1967, 6–18.

NOTES TO CHAPTER 4

1. McGregor, 'The genius of Alcibiades' (cited above), 35.
2. Thuc. VI 60, 1.
3. *Ibid.* 53, 3.
4. *Ibid.* 15, 4.
5. Ar. *Ranae* 1422 sqq.
6. See P. A. Brunt, 'Thucydides and Alcibiades', 62; E. Dele-

becque, *Thucydide et Alcibiade,* 206–7, 232. On Thucydides' analysis of that expedition see most recently W. Liebeschuetz, *Historia* XVII 1968, 289–306.

7. *De Officiis* I 65.

8. *Pol.* 1292a.

9. *Rep.* VIII 562 sqq.

10. *Pol.* 1305a.

11. See Andrewes, *The Greek Tyrants* (1956), 18; W. G. Forrest, *The Emergence of Greek Democracy* (1966), 104–5, 220.

12. *Res Gestae Divi Augusti* 5–6. Cf. Dio Cassius LIV 10; A. H. M. Jones, *Studies in Roman Government and Law* (1960), 12–13 (= *JRS* XLI 1951, 116–17).

13. Cf. P. Geyl, *The Netherlands in the Seventeenth Century* II (1964), 131; eund., *Studies en Strijdschriften* (1958), 152; eund., *History of the Low Countries—Episodes and Problems* (1964), 118–19. William was not apparently implicated in the murder of the de Witts. Cf., e.g., L. J. Rogier, *Geschiedenis der Nederlanden* II (1952), 171.

It may be of interest to note at this point, with a backward glance at Chapter 1, that Hobbes was not without his influence on the propaganda of the de Witt party. See Q. Skinner, *Historical Journal* IX 1966, 289, with note 34.

14. The political aspirations and achievements of Joseph P. Kennedy and his family have been the subject of a very large number of books and articles. The readiness of Americans in general to assume that Robert F. Kennedy was, or ought to be, ready to step into the place left vacant by his murdered brother, President John F. Kennedy, was summed up most succinctly, perhaps, in the title of the book about him by William V. Shannon, *The Heir-Apparent* (1967). See also Theodore H. White, *The Making of the President 1964* (1965), 260: 'There are millions of people all across this country who feel as Robert F. Kennedy does; for them the name of Kennedy is magic, as was the name Stuart under the Hanoverian reign of the Georges; and whenever old or young devotants of the Kennedy loyalty gather, the Bonny Prince Charlie of the faith is Robert F. Kennedy. Like the Jacobites, they await the Restoration.'

I have allowed the text as it was delivered as part of the Martin lectures to stand without alteration, and have made no change in the earlier part of this note. What was then said was tragically corroborated by subsequent events. At the very time of the lectures, Robert Kennedy announced himself a candidate for the Democratic nomination for the Presidency of the United States, and the appeal to the electorate of the name and personality of a Kennedy, like that of the *nomen Caesaris,* was remarkably demonstrated. Two months later, after his victory in the California primary elections, Robert, like his brother John, was the victim of the bullet of an assassin. Without delay or hesitation, comment and speculation turned to what the fourth of the Kennedy brothers, Edward, would do with regard to the presidential campaign. It was not until July 1968 that expectations of his becoming candidate for the Vice-Presidency, in association with the presidential candidature of Vice-President Hubert Humphrey, were laid to rest by Senator Edward Kennedy's denial of any such intention.

At Senator Robert Kennedy's funeral great attention was also paid to the conduct and deportment of his eldest sons, and hopes that they might continue the role of the Kennedy dynasty in public life into the next generation were not disguised.

15. Quintilian, *Inst.* Or. X 1, 98; cf. 88.

16. McGregor, 'The genius of Alcibiades', 27.

17. Thuc. I 138, 3. A really *great* leader has to be able to predict the future with skill and success. See J. de Romilly, *Fondation Hardt—Entretiens* IV (1958), 42–48.

18. Ar. *Ranae* 1425.

19. Cf. Cicero, *De Off.* I 114: 'each man must know his own genius'.

20. Burke, *Thoughts and Details on Scarcity.*

21. *Eth. Nic.* 1123a–1125b.

22. Page 00 above.

23. Burke, *Letter to a Member of the National Assembly.*

24. Plut. *Alc.* 1–7.

25. McGregor, 'The genius of Alcibiades', 28.

26. Lasswell, *Power and Personality* (1948), 16–19, 39–58.

27. See Cic. *De Off.* I 66–67.

28. *Thucydides and His History* (1963), 135–36; cf. McGregor, 'The genius of Alcibiades', 40, and Delebecque, *Thucydide et Alcibiade,* 175. The issue is not taken up in P. A. Brunt's useful article listed above.

29. Arist. *Eth. Nic.* 1124a—ἔοικεν οἷον κόσμος τις εἶναι τῶν ἀρετῶν.

30. References collected in L. Moretti, *Olympionikai* (1956), 109 n. 345.

31. Brunt, 'Thucydides and Alcibiades', 59–65; cf. Delebecque, *Thucydide et Alcibiade,* 227. Both Delebecque and Westlake find two different portraits of Alcibiades in Thucydides' pages, the former interpreting the change in characterisation as primarily due to the personal acquaintance made by the historian with Alcibiades after 412, the latter analysing a development in Thucydides' approach to the problem of personality in his *History.* See also D. J. Stewart, *CJ* LXI 1965–66, 151–52, who in observing the existence of the two portraits rightly points out that they are not contradictory. See J. de Romilly, *Thucydide et l'impérialisme athénien* (1947), 169–72; L. Séchan, *REG* LXXIX 1966, 493–94.

32. Burke, *Letter to the Sheriffs of Bristol.*

33. Plut. *Alc.* 22.

34. McGregor, 'The genius of Alcibiades', 41–43.

35. Burke, *Observations on 'The Present State of the Nation'.*

36. McGregor, 'The genius of Alcibiades', 34–36. On Alcibiades' innocence concerning the mutilation of the Hermae, of which he was evidently not even accused at the time, see D. McDowell, *Andokides 'On the Mysteries'* (1962), 193; K. J. Dover, *Cl. Rev.* n.s. XV 1965, 249.

37. Of the kind which, for example, showed itself in Britain in 1963, in the public reaction to the 'Christine Keeler affair'—a passing scandal which, trivial in itself, had repercussions which did much to undermine confidence in the Conservative administration of Harold Macmillan and to bring a Labour Government into office in the following year.

38. See also A. E. Raubitschek, 'The case against Alcibiades', cited above, 199–201.

39. Sir W. Tarn, *Alexander the Great* II (1948), 324–26.

40. See below, pp. 165–166.

41. Thuc. VI 92, 2–4. For a sympathetic exposition of Alcibiades' action see G. Grote, *History of Greece* (1869 ed.) VII 51 sqq. See also C. Morris, *Western Political Thought* I (1967), 31.

42. Cic. *De Off.* I 119–20.

CHAPTER 5: POWER AND THE MILITARY MACHINE

The following works are referred to below by their authors' names only:

A. H. M. Jones, *Sparta* (1967).

H. Michell, *Sparta* (1952).

P. Roussel, *Sparte,* 2nd ed. (1960).

Also relevant to the material of this chapter are two articles dealing with Sparta in the Thucydidean period:

Preston H. Epps. 'Fear in Spartan character', *Cl. Phil.* XXVIII 1933, 12–29;

H. D. Westlake. 'Alcibiades, Agis and Spartan policy', *JHS* LVIII 1938, 31–40.

NOTES TO CHAPTER 5

1. *Carm.* IV 9, 25–28.

2. Thuc. I 8(¶4)–11.

3. I am inclined to believe that a balance of power achieved between two antithetical groupings of nations (power-blocs) provides one of the most stable power-systems in international affairs. Such a system lacks the fundamental instability of *Kleinstaaterei,* of which fourth-century Greece, with its kaleidoscopic grouping and regrouping of states of roughly commensurate power, is eloquent witness, and for which in more modern times the activities of the countries of southeast Europe provided a name and a warning—Balkanisation. It may even be good for the character and qualities of the nations concerned, as Scipio Nasica urged on a famous occasion (Plut. *Cato Maior* 27; Diod. Sic. XXXIV 33, 3–6; see also D. C. Earl, *The Political Thoughts of Sallust* [1961], 47–50).

The balance achieved in the Pentekontaetea between the Spartan and Athenian blocs, like that in the mid-twentieth century between the members of NATO and the Warsaw Pact nations, produced a workable and stable system, acceptable on both sides so long as parity was maintained. In present circumstances the maintenance of parity depends upon mutual respect for the possession, by each side, of weapons of overwhelmingly destructive capacity—the 'ultimate deterrent'. In Greece such a possibility of balance of terror did not exist, and the Athenians' readiness under Pericles' leadership to seek more than parity, together with Sparta's necessary reaction to it, upset the general stability which mid-fifth-century Hellas briefly enjoyed.

The importance of 'bipolarity' in Greek international politics of the Thucydidean period has been usefully identified and stressed by P. J. Fliess, *Thucydides and the Politics of Bipolarity* (1966); but much of his book is descriptive of the bipolar situation, and he does not derive the further arguments from it of which it is capable. For a judgement to which I subscribe see M. F. McGregor, *Phoenix* XXI 1967, 306–9.

4. Thuc. I 1, 1; 23, 1–2.

5. P. J. Fliess (see n. 3), while also observing this same 'truism that strong and dynamic states normally strive to extend their control over others', concludes that 'oddly enough the drive seems especially pronounced in the bipolar world where it virtually turns into a law of existence' (*ibid.,* 85). This is, in my opinion, to put the issue back to front. We have already remarked that this 'drive' *is* a law of existence. It is, however, only the bipolar world (see n.3) which has some reasonable hope of containing the effects of its operation. In the Pentekontaetia, what Fliess calls 'the stabilization of the bipolar balance' was to some extent achieved by Spartan ἡσυχία coupled with a temporary moderation in that Athenian πλεονεξία which might have been exercised to Sparta's detriment. That is to say, in the fifth-century context of bipolarity, the 'law of existence' was least in evidence. When in the 430's the Athenians began to resume a πολυπραγμοσύνη damaging to the Peloponnesians, the revivification of 'the law' proved ruinous to the bipolar system.

6. IG I² 65; SEG X 72, XIII 10; B. D. Meritt, H. T. Wade-Gery,

M. F. McGregor, *The Athenian Tribute Lists (ATL)* II (1949), 52–53 D.8; see also *ATL* III (1950), 142–48.

7. Thuc. I 98, 4. On the meaning of δουλεία in this context see *ATL* III (1950), 155–57; J. de Romilly, *Thucydide et l'impérialisme athénien* (1947), 90; A. W. Gomme, *A Historical Commentary on Thucydides* III (1956), 646.

8. Von Clausewitz, *On War,* bk. II ch. 3.

9. *Ibid.,* bk. III ch. 4.

10. See the figures given (with all proper hesitation) by V. Ehrenberg in *The Greek State* (1960), 33.

11. Xen. *Resp. Lac.* I 1. On Spartan ὀλιγανθρωπία and Spartan population generally see Michell, *Sparta* 228–32, Jones, *Sparta* 129–37.

12. Arist. *Politics* 1270a.

13. H. D. F. Kitto, *The Greeks* (1951), 91.

14. See Plut. *Lycurgus* 30, Isocrates VIII *(De Pace),* 102–5.

15. Arist. *Politics* 1270a; Plut. *Lycurgus* 14.

16. *Resp. Lac.* XIV 3.

17. *Ibid.* I 1. On the Spartan system of education see Michell, 165–204; Jones, 34–39; Roussel, 45–52, Kitto, *The Greeks,* 91–95, H. I. Marrou, *A History of Education in Antiquity,* Eng. ed. (1956), 14–25. Indeed, any good general account of Sparta in particular or of Greece as a whole cannot omit some discussion of it. The analysis of certain details by W. den Boer in *Laconian Studies* (1954), 233–298, is especially to be recommended; and on family life see now W. K. Lacey, *The Family in Classical Greece* (1968), 194–208. For a brief and well-pointed exposition of the Spartan situation as here described see M. I Finley, *The Ancient Greeks* (1963), 65–66.

18. See Isocrates VIII *(De Pace)* 116–19.

19. Xen. *Resp. Lac.* IV 5; see also Roussel, 70–71.

20. There is little need in this context to elaborate bibliographically concerning the Spartan alliances, usually referred to as the 'Peloponnesian League.' See most conveniently Jones, 44–47, Roussel, 83–88. The 'basic' articles on the subject are still those of J. A. O. Larsen in *Cl. Phil.* XXVII 1932, 136–50; XXVIII 1933, 257–76; XXIX 1934, 1–19; see the same author's *Representative Government in Greek and Roman History* (1955), 47–65.

21. Thuc. I 76, 2.

22. The argument thus tends to confirm Thucydides' analysis of the war's ἀληθεστάτη πρόφασις (I 23, 6).

23. Thuc. I 10, 2. See above, p. 37.

24. Thuc. I 68–71, from which the sentiments of the next few sentences are derived.

25. Von Clausewitz, *On War*, bk. I ch. 1.

26. *Il Principe*, 13.

27. Thuc. I 121, 3.

28. *Ibid.* 86.

29. See J. H. Finley, *Thucydides* (1947), 92 and 300–1.

30. See Thuc. I 42, 2: τὸ τε γὰρ ξυμφέρον ἐν ᾧ ἄν τις ἐλάχιστα ἁμαρτάνῃ μάλιστα ἕπεται.

31. Thuc. IV 55, 3-4. This is not an easy phrase to render. It does not really amount to 'abject terror', 'utter distraction', or even, more mildly, 'complete dismay'. Ἔκπληξις carries the basic sense of being knocked or put off one's stroke, and thence refers to the bewilderment or consternation which may result from such an event. Thus 'their morale collapsed' (R. Warner) or 'they were panic-stricken' (B. Jowett), while spirited translations, do not wholly reflect the essence of Thucydides' comment.

32. Preston H. Epps, 'Fear in Spartan character'. P. J. Fliess in *Thucydides and the Politics of Bipolarity*, without referring to Epps's article, independently emphasises the timidity as well as the rigidity of the Spartan character (140–43; see also 59–60).

33. Thuc. IV 40.

34. Thuc. V 75, 3.

35. Von Clausewitz, *On War*, bk. II ch. 4.

36. Sir Basil Liddell Hart, *Thoughts on War* (1944), 20.

37. *Hellenica* I 1, 23.

38. Liddell Hart, *Thoughts on War*, 178.

39. *Ibid.*, 179.

40. Thuc. I 122, 1; VI 91, 6.

41. Thuc. VIII 80, 1-2.

42. *Ibid.* 8, 2.

43. *Ibid.* 22 et sqq.

44. *Ibid.* 106, 2 and 5.

45. *Ibid.* 1, 3; 95, 2; 96, 1–2.
46. *Ibid.* 5, 1.
47. *Ibid.* 96.
48. *Ibid.* 2, 3.
49. *Ibid.* 2, 4.
50. *Ibid.* 15.
51. *Ibid.* 5, 3.
52. *Il Principe,* 25. Cf. K. Reinhardt, *Von Werken und Formen* (1948), 240–1.
53. Thuc. II 13, 2.

CHAPTER 6: THE GREAT POWER

The following articles are of particular interest in connexion with much of the material of this chapter:
A. Andrewes. 'Thucydides and the Persians', *Historia* X 1961, 1–18.
J. M. Cook. 'The problem of Classical Ionia', *Proc. Camb. Phil. Soc.* n.s. VII 1961, 9–18.

NOTES TO CHAPTER 6

1. A. G. Woodhead, *The Greeks in the West* (1962), 118–20.
2. See M. Cary, *Cambridge Ancient History* VI, 55–56.
3. Xenophanes fr. 22 (Edmonds): Theognis 764, 775–79.
4. Aeschylus, *Persae* 1–92.
5. Her. VII 184–87. The vast army took seven days and seven nights, he tells us, to cross the Hellespont (VII 56), and on its march it drank whole rivers dry (VII 21). See also VII 43, 108, 127, 196.
It is worth dwelling on these details not, as is generally done, in order to argue a scholarly scepticism concerning their historical veracity but in order to share the state of mind with which the Greeks viewed the Persian approach. To search for historical truth about it is only one aspect of the study of an historical period. There is no less importance, for an understanding of the same period, in

what was thought at the time, however erroneously, to be true, and so became influential in shaping reaction and consequent action.

6. Her. VII 187.

7. On the *angoscia corale* of the Greeks see G. Maddoli, *La Parola del Passato* XVIII 1963, 425. It is arguable that too little attention has been paid in work on the Persian Wars to this aspect of the matter, the authors being more concerned to discuss the political and military situation and the mechanics and details of the preparations made by both sides.

C. Hignett (*Xerxes' Invasion of Greece* [1963], 90–94), it may here be mentioned, was far too sanguine in his assessment of the relative strength and weakness of the Greeks and the Persians through undue neglect of this factor. He claimed that only to a superficial observer would the Greeks appear to be inescapably doomed. But the priests of Delphic Apollo, who had reached this conclusion, were far from being superficial observers of the Greek scene; on the contrary, they were in as good a position as anyone to reach a just appraisal of the matter. Most of their contemporaries will in their heart of hearts have been as pessimistic as they, even if they showed themselves less realistic, in their determination to offer resistance notwithstanding the predictable result. Pierre Lévêque's phrase referring to the 'thoughtless Medism' of Delphi (*The Greek Adventure* [1968], 233) is unhappily chosen. Only memories of Marathon will have offered a pale gleam of hope, but the vast scale of Xerxes' preparations must have given the impression that Marathon had been too trivial, in comparison, to serve as grounds for confident optimism.

8. Thuc. I 69, 5.

9. See Thuc. I 96, 1. On the original intention of the Delian League see most recently R. Sealey, *Ancient Society and Institutions: Studies Presented to Victor Ehrenberg on his 75th Birthday*, 1966, 237–42. The 'standard references' are J. A. O. Larsen, *HSCP* LI 1940, 175–213; B. D. Meritt, H. T. Wade-Gery, M. F. McGregor, *The Athenian Tribute Lists* III (1950), 225–33. But any account of fifth-century Athens, or indeed of fifth-century Greece in general, devotes some attention to this matter.

10. Thuc. II 67; see also I 83, 1–2.

11. Thuc. IV 50.

12. Andocides III 29; IG II² 8 (= SEG XIX 16). See H. T. Wade-Gery, *Essays in Greek History* (1958), 207–11. A. E. Raubitschek, however, prefers to date this treaty shortly before the expedition to Sicily in 415 (*Greek, Roman and Byzantine Studies* V 1964, 156–57).

13. Ar. *Ach.* 61–128.

14. See Thuc. I 73, 5.

15. Thuc. VIII 5, 5.

16. See Her. VI 42, 2; E. M. Walker, *Cambridge Ancient History* V, 470.

17. Thuc. I 69, 4.

18. See Ar. *Eq.* 174, 1303–4; Plut. *Per.* 20, *Alcib.* 17.

19. Thuc. VIII 18, 37, 58.

20. See B. D. Meritt, *Cl. Phil.* LXI 1966, 182–84; A. H. M. Jones, *Sparta* (1967), 84–86; V. Ehrenberg, *From Solon to Socrates* (1968), 306–9 and 458 nn. 93 and 95–96. For the texts and further references to modern discussions see H. Bengtson, *Die Staatsverträge des Altertums* II—*die Verträge der griechisch-römischen Welt von 700 bis 338 v. Chr.* (1962), 138–43 nn. 200–2.

21. Wade-Gery, *Essays in Greek History* (1958), 212.

22. Thuc. V 18, 5.

23. Cook, 'The problem of Classical Ionia' (see above).

24. In its basic nature a Greek *polis* consisted, indeed, of a built-up area (ἄστυ) together with the agricultural land surrounding it. For a succinct description see V. Ehrenberg, *The Greek State* (1960), 28–32. It was unusual for this land to be as extensive as it was in the case of the Athenian city-state, where the *politai* lived not only in the *asty* but in more than 150 small population-groupings (the country demes) outside it covering the whole of Attica (roughly 1000 square miles of territory).

Where a city's extra-urban possessions were particularly extensive, a distinction could be made between the home-territory (πολιτικὴ χώρα) and the rest, as happened at Sparta, and the conditions of tenure under which the land was held and farmed by the *politai* might differ as between the two categories. The usufruct or even the possession of the city's χώρα might be denied to the *politai* by the intervention of some outside agency. For such *Poleis ohne Territorium* see F. Hampl, *Klio* XXXII 1939, 1–60, F. Gschnitzer, *Abhängige Orte im griechischen Altertum* (1958), 159–72.

The juridical position of the city-lands vis-à-vis the cities themselves in Ionia caused difficulties when the Ionians were 'liberated' by Alexander the Great in 334–3, and continued to present problems under the Hellenistic monarchies. See, for example, the issues dealt with by Ehrenberg, *Alexander and the Greeks* (1938), 1–51, and *The Greek State* (1960), 191–205; Sir W. Tarn, *Alexander the Great* II (1950), 199–227.

25. Cook, 'The problem of Classical Ionia', 17.

26. The acceptance came a little wryly from the more conservative, who had been less favourably disposed towards Russia in the inter-war period; but the expediency of the *rapprochement* was reinforced by the general and genuine admiration for the Russians' heroic resistance, and was gradually transformed into a recognition that the Russian system had some merits (for the Russians, and provided that there was no effort to export them), and that a *modus vivendi* in the postwar world would to a considerable degree depend on continuing co-operation between Russia and the West. The sentiments of Winston Churchill at the time might indeed have been comparable with those of an Athenian statesman during the Archidamian War advocating a deal with Persia, when he affirmed that, if Hitler invaded Hell itself, he would at least make a favourable reference to the Devil in the House of Commons.

27. Dem. XIV *(On the Symmories)* 3–13; XV *(On the Freedom of the Rhodians)* 5–10.

28. M. N. Tod, *Greek Historical Inscriptions* II (1948), 145; SEG XI 318, XXII 265 (all with full bibliography).

29. *Hellenica* III iv, 19.

30. See R. Andreotti, *Historia* V 1956, 257–66; O. Reverdin, *Fondation Hardt—Entretiens* VIII (1962), 104–5.

31. Andrewes, 'Thucydides and the Persians' (see above).

32. Thuc. VIII 28.

33. Thuc. III 31, 2.
34. *Ibid.* 34.
35. See Andrewes, 'Thucydides and the Persians', 4–5.
36. Thuc. I 115, 4.
37. See Andocides III 29.
38. Thuc. VIII 28, 2.
39. *BSA LII* 1957, 104–5.
40. *Epist.* I 10, 24.

CHAPTER 7: POWER AND PUBLIC OPINION

The following articles are of particular relevance to this chapter:
A. Andrewes. 'The Melian Dialogue and Perikles' last speech,' *Proc. Camb. Phil. Soc.* n.s. VI 1960, 1–10.

————'The Mytilene Debate: Thucydides III 36–49', *Phoenix* XVI 1962, 64–85.

L. Pearson. 'Popular ethics in the world of Thucydides', *Cl. Phil.* LII 1957, 228–44.

R. P. Winnington-Ingram. 'Τὰ δέοντα εἰπεῖν: Cleon and Diodotus', *Bulletin of the Institute of Classical Studies, University of London,* no. 12, 1965, 70–82.

NOTES TO CHAPTER 7

*Reprinted by permission of *The Village Voice*. Copyrighted by The Village Voice Inc.

1. Plato, *Rep.* I, 330d–336a. See L. Pearson (above), esp. 230. I do not, however, agree with Pearson's thesis that the Thucydidean period showed a general decline of standard in regard to respect for pledged undertakings. Thucydides may have thought that it did and may have conveyed (and hoped to convey) such an impression, but his narrative shows that the same standards of conduct are effectively in operation throughout his *History*. Development takes place only in the growing lack of concealment of the real character of those standards. See further in nn. 10 and 17 below.

2. See F. M. Cornford, *The Republic of Plato* (1941), 11–12. The view of Gorgias quoted by Meno (Plato, *Meno* 71e) is very similar

to that of Polemarchus, which must not therefore be dismissed as the naïveté of an amateur produced only in order to be scornfully refuted.

3. See R. P. Winnington-Ingram, 'Tὰ δέοντα εἰπεῖν' (above), 73; A. W. H. Adkins, *Merit and Responsibility* (1960), 269; Thuc. I 86.

4. Plato, *Laches* 190e.

5. Plato, *Charmides* 159b. On *sophrosyne* in general see Helen North, *TAPA* LXXVIII 1947, 1–17, and *Sophrosyne* (1966), a work already quoted above in matters of detail (on the argument of the *Charmides* see esp. 153–58).

It is worth noting that in Thucydides such phrases as εἰ σωφρονοῦμεν or σωφρονεῖσθε (e.g., VI 11, 7) carry this connotation of deliberate orderliness: 'if we (or you) pause to reflect in a deliberate manner'. To that extent, North's translation (*ibid.*, 109) of ἤν γε σωφρόνως βουλεύησθε as 'if you take thought for your own advantage' seems to me mistaken. Nor is 'if you take a sensible view of the matter' or 'if you use good judgement' much better. The real sense is 'if you really sit down and think the matter through in an orderly way'. Thucydides' *sophrones* are not only 'right-thinking' people; they combine orderliness of thought with orderliness of conduct. Ὕβρις, on the contrary, reveals disorder in both; see North, 91, with n. 22 and references.

Thucydides' regard for σωφροσύνη and εὐνομία, its product, is embodied in his implicitly favourable portrayal of King Archidamus (see F. M. Wassermann, *CJ* XLVIII 1952–53, 193–200; R. Reimer-Klaas, *Macht und Recht bei Thukydides* (diss. 1959), 28–29) and is not absent from the Funeral Speech, which attempts to combine these virtues with the elements of democracy (see J. H. Oliver, *Rhein. Mus.* XCVIII 1955, 37–40).

6. Tac., *Agr.* 30, 6.

7. Plato, *Protagoras* 351b.

8. L. Pearson, *Popular Ethics in Ancient Greece* (1962), 172–73; Dem. XV 28.

9. Thuc. V 89.

10. It is perhaps this new readiness to be frank about the matter which gives the false impression of a 'decline of standard' (see n. 1).

It is a frankness which makes modern readers and critics themselves feel uncomfortable and thus disposed to think in terms of degeneration. But, as Wassermann has pointed out, it was a frankness shared in essentials with Euripides and Socrates (*TAPA* LXXVIII 1947, 19; see also J. H. Finley, *HSCP* XLIX 1938, 23–68).

11. Pearson, *Popular Ethics in Ancient Greece*, 162.

12. See above p. 35. See also C. Morris, *Western Political Thought* I (1967), 39.

13. For example, by F. M. Cornford, *Thucydides Mythistoricus* (1907), esp. 181–87, F. M. Wassermann, *TAPA* LXXVIII 1947, 18–36.

14. As Sir Ernest Barker suggested; see pp. 3–4 above.

15. See Winnington-Ingram, 'Τὰ δέοντα εἰπεῖν', 71–75, A. Andrewes, *Phoenix* XVI 1962, 72–73, R. Reimer-Klaas, *Macht und Recht bei Thukydides* (diss. 1959), 106–7.

16. Thuc. III 36, 4. On the ἀναψήφισις see K. J. Dover, *JHS* LXXV 1955, 17–20.

17. This, although often observed (see most recently V. Ehrenberg, *From Solon to Socrates* [1968], 268), needs to be emphasised, since readers would prefer to believe that humanitarianism was indeed the main issue in the debate. See, for example, H. North, *Sophrosyne*, 108, where the author regards Diodotus' success 'in persuading the assembly to revoke the cruel decree' as showing that 'the moral decay of Athens is still in its early stages'. There is nothing 'moral' on either side in the whole debate, as it is recorded by Thucydides, and the repeal of the first decision, as persuaded by Diodotus, was founded entirely on considerations of advantage. Because of this deliberate exclusion of any 'moral' argument it might indeed be argued that the 'moral decay' had already set in, i.e., that it is to be regarded as a Periclean and not a post-Periclean phenomenon. Such a contention would bring further problems of its own in our and Thucydides' interpretation of Periclean Athens, but on that basis the views commonly held that the war represents a history of Athenian deterioration would lack substance. Conversely, a city which could enact and hold by the amnesty of 403 can hardly be accused of lack of moral sense.

I believe, in sum, that the same essential aspects of 'national character' were present in Athens before the war as after it. The terminology and cross-currents of thought revealed in the kind of argument so often brought to bear upon Athenian 'moral conduct' in this period serve to underline the difficulties which modern critics face in clearing their own minds of the predispositions inherent in them before they can get to grips with the world of Thucydides.

18. Thuc. III 37, 2.

19. Thuc. VIII 48, 4.

20. Pearson, *Popular Ethics in Ancient Greece*, 160.

21. Thuc. VIII 66. See also Thuc. IV 86, 6, where Brasidas regards ἀπάτη εὐπρεπής as αἴσχιον than βία ἐμφάνης, at least for a man of quality, on the interesting grounds that the latter is a more manly and open assertion of power which carries its own justification, while tricks which hide a raw deal in a fine package, although evidence of the γνώμη of their author, smack of ἀδικία. On this argument he would presumably, had he lived, have found himself compelled to endorse the sentiments of the Athenians expressed in the Melian Dialogue.

22. Conversely, when a régime has been 'liberalised', as in the period of 'de-Stalinisation' and of the loosening of the bonds linking the Communist governments of Eastern Europe very closely with Russia, much trouble has been taken to expose the same trials as 'unjust' and to see to it that the authors of them are brought to book. The same requirements are here at work, under the unnecessary impulse of the same necessity.

23. Thuc. VIII 86, 4.

24. Thuc. VI 16–17.

25. Thuc. VIII 48, 4.

26. Thuc. VI 89–92.

27. Pearson, *Popular Ethics in Ancient Greece*, 159.

28. See R. Seager, *Historia* XVI 1967, 6–18, esp. 16, who rightly emphasises that all other charges levelled at Alcibiades (and in particular the charge that he aimed to become tyrant) arose from dislike of his ἐπιτηδεύματα. That power must take cognizance of traditional morality is properly taken into account by Machiavelli,

for the existence of such morality is a fact of the political world. 'Men in general are as much affected by what things seem to be as by what they are; often indeed they are moved more by the appearance than by the reality of things'(*Discorsi* I, 25). Men of political virtuosity who comprehend what lies beneath the surface and who demand the substance rather than the shadow of power learn to convert these appearances to their own uses. See Hanna H. Gray, *The Responsibility of Power: Historical Essays in honor of Hajo Holborn* (1967), 48.

Alcibiades' political virtuosity contained the flaw that he was too careless of this important factor, and he paid the penalty for his carelessness. He would have agreed with Machiavelli as to the basic truth that traditional ethics are in themselves no guide to the acquisition, use, or maintenance of power.

29. On Greek patriotism in general, and on that of Alcibiades in particular, see N. M. Pusey's useful article 'Alcibiades and τὸ φιλόπολι' in *HSCP* LI 1940, 215–31. Pusey sought to 'quarrel with the belief that the ancient Greeks of the classical period were bound to their city-states by a passionate patriotic attachment', taking Sir Alfred Zimmern (*The Greek Commonwealth*⁵ [1931], 67) as representative of that mistaken orthodoxy. It emerges from Pusey's analysis that it is very difficult to find Athenians or other Greeks 'whose political actions are consistent with the modern conception of the patriot'. There is thus not the 'distortion' in Alcibiades' use of the word 'patriotism' which Finley, for example, claims (*Thucydides,* 232). One might go so far as to suggest that Alcibiades' conduct was, by Greek standards, reasonable and acceptable, and fully open to justification along the lines by which he sought to justify it. It demonstrated to the Athenians not an example of unpatriotic behaviour which they might regard as shocking but a crowning instance of Alcibiades' complete unreliability as far as their own ὠφελία was concerned.

The issue, in any assessment of Alcibiades, is an important one, but it was not effectively raised by M. F. McGregor (*Phoenix* XIX 1965, 27–46) nor, in what is still the standard work on him, by Jean Hatzfeld (*Alcibiade*², 1951).

30. See N. M. Pusey's conclusion (*ibid.*, 229) that 'our notion of patriotism, as a feeling distinguished from mere love for a physical city, had small power to influence Greek citizens for good or bad', nor did it play any considerable role in their society.

31. See [Xen.], 'Aθ. Πολ. II 17.

32. Thuc. VIII 1, 1.

33. Thuc. II 54, 4.

34. See F. M. Wassermann, *TAPA* LXXVIII 1947, 31.

35. Thuc. II 47, 4.

36. On the nature of Thucydidean ἀνάγκη I agree in essentials with the interpretation of P. A. Brunt. See the excellent preface to his abridgement of Jowett's translation of Thucydides, 1963, xxx–xxxi, and *Cl. Rev.* n.s. XVII 1967, 279; see also J. de Romilly, *Thucydide et l'impérialisme athénien* (1947), 260–68.

37. Thuc. V 105. On the ἀνάγκη φύσεως in later fifth-century thought, see R. Reimer-Klaas, *Macht und Recht*, 70–72.

38. See, for example, J. H. Finley, *Thucydides*, 312–15; J. de Romilly, *Thucydide*, 149–52; F. M. Wassermann, *TAPA* LXXVIII 1947, 29–31.

39. Thuc. II 61, 3–4.

40. See J. de Romilly, *Thucydide*, 268–74.

41. See Leo Strauss, *Thoughts on Machiavelli* (1958), 292; 'The fate of neither Cesare Borgia nor Manlius Capitolinus is tragic or understood by Machiavelli as tragic. They failed because they had chance or the times against them. As regards chance in general, it can be conquered; man is the master.'

Thucydides did not view the matter so uncompromisingly. H. Herter argued that in his judgement the truly gifted statesman (represented by Pericles) can indeed conquer τύχη with his γνώμη: see *Rhein. Mus.* XCIII 1949–50, 133–53, *Studies Presented to David Moore Robinson* II (1953), 613–23. But it may be doubted whether Thucydides went as far as that. He does not set γνώμη *against* τύχη. Chance *can* be conquered, indeed, but man is never the absolute master; he can only mitigate, sometimes with reasonably complete success, chance's free operation. Thus γνώμη and τύχη, although *prima facie* in opposition, are not necessarily so and may, in producing a given result, be complementary. See A. Cizek, *Studii Clasice* IX 1967, 46.

42. Thuc. IV 17, 4–5, 18, 3–5. See Ian Trethowan, *The Times* (London), 30 March 1967: 'All politicians know that luck can play an almost frighteningly large part in their lives'.

43. H. R. Veltfort and G. E. Lee, *Journal of Abnormal and Social Psychology* XXXVIII, 1943, Suppl., 138–54. See also N. J. Smelser, *Theory of Collective Behaviour* (1962), 223. On the scapegoat complex in general there were interesting remarks by R. Blake in *Illustrated London News,* 22 April 1967, 14.

Index